GRACE ABOUNDING

INTERNATIONAL THEOLOGICAL COMMENTARY

Fredrick Carlson Holmgren and George A. F. Knight
General Editors

GRACE ABOUNDING

A Commentary on the Book of

Hosea

H. D. BEEBY

WM. B. EERDMANS PUBLISHING CO., GRAND RAPIDS

THE HANDSEL PRESS LTD, EDINBURGH

Copyright © 1989 by William B. Eerdmans Publishing Company
First published 1989 by William B. Eerdmans Publishing Company,
255 Jefferson Ave. S.E., Grand Rapids, Michigan 49503
and
The Handsel Press Limited
33 Montgomery Street, Edinburgh EH7 5JX

Library of Congress Cataloging-in-Publication Data

Beeby, H. D.
Grace abounding: a commentary on the Book of Hosea / H. D. Beeby.
p.   cm.   —(International theological commentary)
Bibliography: p. 189
ISBN 0-8028-0430-6
1. Bible. O.T. Hosea—Commentaries. I. Title. II. Series.
BS1565.3.B34   1989
224'.607—dc20   89-1469
CIP

Handsel Press ISBN 0 905312 95 3

CONTENTS

CONTENTS

IV: PAST, PRESENT, AND FUTURE: ON TO THE KNOWLEDGE OF GOD

EDITORS' PREFACE

The Old Testament alive in the Church: this is the goal of the *International Theological Commentary*. Arising out of changing, unsettled times, this Scripture speaks with an authentic voice to our own troubled world. It witnesses to God's ongoing purpose and to his caring presence in the universe without ignoring those experiences of life that cause one to question his existence and love. This commentary series is written by front-rank scholars who treasure the life of faith.

Addressed to ministers and Christian educators, the *International Theological Commentary* moves beyond the usual critical-historical approach to the Bible and offers a *theological* interpretation of the Hebrew text. Thus, engaging larger textual units of the biblical writings, the authors of these volumes assist the reader in the appreciation of the theology underlying the text as well as its place in the thought of the Hebrew Scriptures. But more, since the Bible is the book of the believing community, its text has acquired ever more meaning through an ongoing interpretation. This growth of interpretation may be found both within the Bible itself and in the continuing scholarship of the Church.

Contributors to the *International Theological Commentary* are Christians—persons who affirm the witness of the New Testament concerning Jesus Christ. For Christians, the Bible is *one* scripture containing the Old and New Testaments. For this reason, a commentary on the Old Testament may not ignore the second part of the canon, namely, the New Testament.

Since its beginning, the Church has recognized a special relationship between the two Testaments. But the precise character of this bond has been difficult to define. Thousands of books and articles have discussed the issue. The diversity of views represented in these publications makes us aware that the Church is not of one mind in expressing the "how" of this relationship. The authors of this commentary share a developing consensus that any serious explanation of the Old Testament's relationship to the New will uphold the integrity of the Old Testament. Even though Christianity is rooted in the soil of the Hebrew Scriptures, the biblical interpreter must take care lest he or she "christianize" these Scriptures.

Authors writing in this commentary will, no doubt, hold varied views concerning *how* the Old Testament relates to the New. No attempt has been made to dictate one viewpoint in this matter. With the whole Church, we are convinced that the relationship between the two Testaments is real and substantial. But we recognize also the diversity of opinions among Christian scholars when they attempt to articulate fully the nature of this relationship.

In addition to the Christian Church, there exists another people for whom the Old Testament is important, namely, the Jewish community. Both Jews and Christians claim the Hebrew Bible as Scripture. Jews believe that the basic teachings of this Scripture point toward, and are developed by, the Talmud, which assumed its present form about A.D. 500. On the other hand, Christians hold that the Old Testament finds its fulfillment in the New Testament. The Hebrew Bible, therefore, belongs to both the Church and the Synagogue.

Recent studies have demonstrated how profoundly early Christianity reflects a Jewish character. This fact is not surprising because the Christian movement arose out of the context of first-century Judaism. Further, Jesus himself was Jewish, as were the first Christians. It is to be expected, therefore, that Jewish and Christian interpretations of the Hebrew Bible will reveal similarities *and* disparities. Such is the case. The authors of the *International Theological Commentary* will refer to the various Jewish traditions that they consider important for an appreciation of the Old Testament text. Such references will enrich our understanding of certain biblical passages and, as an extra gift, offer us insight into the relationship of Judaism to early Christianity.

An important second aspect of the present series is its *international* character. In the past, Western church leaders were considered to be *the* leaders of the Church—at least by those living in the West! The theology and biblical exegesis done by these scholars dominated the thinking of the Church. Most commentaries were produced in the Western world and reflected the lifestyle, needs, and thoughts of its civilization. But the Christian Church is a worldwide community. People who belong to this universal Church reflect differing thoughts, needs, and lifestyles.

Today the fastest growing churches in the world are to be found, not in the West, but in Africa, Indonesia, South America, Korea, Taiwan, and elsewhere. By the end of this century, Christians in these areas will outnumber those who live in the West. In our age, especially, a commentary on the Bible must transcend the parochialism of Western civilization and be sensitive to issues that are the special problems of persons who live outside of the "Christian" West, issues such as race relations, personal survival and fulfillment, liberation, revolution, famine, tyranny, disease, war, the poor, religion and state. Inspired of God, the authors of the Old Testament knew what life is like on the edge of existence. They addressed themselves to everyday people who often faced more than everyday problems. Refusing to limit God to the "spiritual," they portrayed him as one who heard and knew the cries of people in pain (see Exod. 3:7-8). The contributors to the *International Theological Commentary* are persons who prize the writings of these biblical authors as a word of life to our world today. They read the Hebrew Scriptures in the twin contexts of ancient Israel and our modern day.

The scholars selected as contributors underscore the international aspect of the series. Representing very different geographical, ideological, and ecclesiastical backgrounds, they come from more than seventeen countries. Besides scholars from such traditional countries as England, Scotland, France, Italy, Switzerland, Canada, New Zealand, Australia, South Africa, and the United States, contributors from the following places are included: Israel, Indonesia, India, Thailand, Singapore, Taiwan, and countries of Eastern Europe. Such diversity makes for richness of thought. Christian scholars living in Buddhist, Muslim, or Socialist lands may be able to offer the World Church insights into the biblical message—insights to which the scholarship of the West could be blind.

The proclamation of the biblical message is the focal concern of the *International Theological Commentary*. Generally speaking, the authors of these commentaries value the historical-critical studies of past scholars, but they are convinced that these studies by themselves are not enough. The Bible is more than an object of critical study; it is the revelation of God. In the written Word, God has disclosed himself and his will to humankind. Our authors see themselves as servants of the Word which, when rightly received, brings *shalom* to both the individual and the community.

Dr. H. D. Beeby lived in China and Taiwan from 1946 to 1972. For most of that time he was Professor of the Old Testament in Tainan Theological College, Taiwan, and only ceased to hold that position because of his expulsion by the Nationalist Government of Taiwan.

—George A. F. Knight
—Fredrick Carlson Holmgren

INTRODUCTION

One function of an introduction to a prophetic book is to place it in its historical background. For a book like Hosea, this usually means a total concentration on the 8th cent. B.C., as the prophet Hosea belongs to that century. While not quarreling with an 8th cent. date for Hosea or with the provision—to a degree—of this type of context, it is essential to point out that the book of Hosea as we have it cannot and should not be read only in the context of northern Israel in the 8th cent. B.C. Its true context is much wider.

The words of Hosea were heard in Judah a generation after they were uttered in Galilee, and were there modified to meet Judah's needs at that time. Succeeding generations continued to hear things from his words which only their particular contexts could call forth. So the book which the Jewish community and later the Church has bequeathed to us is one which was preserved, not only for what it said in the context of the 8th cent., but even more for what it said against the background of, for example, the 2nd cent. B.C. and the 4th cent. A.D., the dates when it passed into the canons of the Jewish and Christian Bibles. Yet even these are not the most significant contexts; the book would be a dead word of a dead God if they were. The living word of the living God in the book of Hosea must finally be heard against the background of, and in response to the needs of, the reader's own time.

HOSEA'S TIME

Hosea was active in the third quarter of the 8th cent. B.C. When he began to prophesy, Jeroboam II (786-746) was still on the throne. When he ceased, the fall of the northern kingdom of Israel was imminent. His career, therefore, stretched from times of prosperity and comparative stability through to the instability of toppling dynasties, social unrest, warfare, vacillating leadership, and partial subjugation to humiliation and the shadow of final disaster. All this is reflected in the contents of the book, arranged roughly in chronological order. The political background of Hosea's day will be dealt with in the body of the Commentary; the religious situation merits some mention in the Introduction.

Beginning with Gen. 12:6 and especially in the book of Judges, the biblical authors leave us in no doubt that the Canaanites were still in the land. And with the Canaanites there remained the Canaanite religion. This was both a parallel religion with its own cult and also a strong influence on the Yahweh cult, which to a very great extent had suffered from a wrong kind of indigenization. Hosea's main attack was directed towards this disastrous syncretistic mixture which threatened to distort and possibly engulf the faith once delivered to Moses.

The Canaanite religion was based on nature myths which laid great stress on fertility and little if any on morality. The resulting cult was a technique for ensuring that everything that could be fruitful and multiply did so with the least difficulty and the greatest dispatch. This religion was for the Canaanites (and for most of the Israelites) what scientific humanism and technology are for people of the 20th century: essential to the means of production and for ensuring regular increase in the Gross National Product.

Instead of one God the Canaanites had more like seventy gods. Once El had been the supreme deity, but a celestial palace revolution had replaced El by Baal, and for Hosea Baal symbolized all that was erroneous and corrupt. Most likely the word *ba'al* originally meant "the one who fructifies" — the one capable of making the other fertile. The husband, the bull, and perhaps the rain were therefore *ba'als*. The power to fructify carried with it authority, and therefore the word had come to mean "the one with authority," or "lord" or "master." Myths about fertility, used to foster fertility, inevitably engendered cultic techniques which gave prominence to sexual acts designed to operate with the powers of imitative magic. Male and female prostitutes thronged the shrines, making sanctuaries indistinguishable from brothels and holiness indistinguishable from harlotry. The faith of Hosea's fathers had become so debased that in almost every respect it was now the opposite of the great original. So Hosea is called to state the case for the prosecution and eventually to ascend the bench and don the black cap.

Hosea Himself

We roughly know Hosea's dates; we are told his father's name, that he married and had three children, and that his "accent" (like Peter's) tells us he is a northerner. Beyond this we rely only on guesswork based upon the material in Hosea's own preaching; and as this comes to us through the most confused Hebrew text in the OT, the guessing can be hazardous. The prophet's use of imagery and metaphor have prompted some to compare him with Jesus. The names Hosea and Jesus come from the same Hebrew root. Hosea's birthplace cannot have been too far from Nazareth; perhaps lyrical imagery flourished in the fair hills of Galilee so that they were but two of a long line of lakeland poets. Hosea was knowledgeable about the tradition of his people and about contemporary history as well. This however does not make him a scholar by profession; the profusion of kitchen metaphors in his book may even point to his having been a cook or baker.

The details of Hosea's family life are unlikely to be imaginary, but they are given to us as a series of events brought about by God's commands as a means of manifesting God's wishes and making the Word of God visible and tangible as well as audible. Biographical or autobiographical details are noticeably absent. Hosea the man is suppressed to clear the stage for Hosea the prophet of Yahweh.

Clues to be Followed in the Commentary

Other clues to Hosea and his prophecy will follow in the Commentary itself. The following points have guided the writer and no doubt will help the reader.

1. *"Borrowing from the Enemy"*

Hosea is called to battle against polytheism, sexuality in heavenly places, and debauchery on earth. To the Israelites the idea of Yahweh having a consort was so unthinkable that their language did not even possess a word for "goddess." Yet onto this bordello battlefield was propelled no virgin knight in shining armor but a man whom God had married off to a prostitute. And what is even more astounding is that his banner bore the strange device, "God has a wife." In the boldest example of cultural borrowing in the OT,

Hosea turned the weapons of the enemy against the enemy host. Divine marriage and fertility symbolism were baptized into a crusade against Canaanite religion which was based upon the symbolism of divine marriage and fertility. If Hosea had known the expressions "set a thief to catch a thief" or "a hair of the dog that bit you," he might well have quoted them!

2. Recapitulation of Basic Themes

The Western mind likes its literature to move in steady progression from beginning to middle to end. The logical argument and its historical development are its main tests of unity. Other cultures have other ways of thinking and therefore other ways of writing. Not surprisingly, their sense of unity manifests itself in a variety of ways. The unity of the book of Hosea consists of several contributory unities, one of them satisfying Western norms by beginning with the marriage (or the election of Israel at Sinai) and concluding with the salvation of Israel in the future; the others, however, are less obvious, while two of them merit special mention.

The first of these patterns is that of recapitulation. Hosea has one basic sermon or set of themes, and these themes appear and reappear throughout the book; the book as a whole has thus been fashioned to make its overall structure conform to these same themes. The clearest statement of the themes is to be found in Hos. 11—a good place to begin the study of the book. There in outline is the word of the LORD which came to Hosea. God chose Israel and showered her with grace abounding. Israel's response was rebellion and more sin. This drew from God the just condemnation and the punishment that such rebellion deserves. Unable to learn from her history, Israel is destined to repeat it; she must go back into bondage. But God is God and therefore gracious. God's last word is a word of compassion and restoration. The God who reigns is the God who saves. This basic scheme is never far from us; the numerous recapitulations of it will be pointed to in the Commentary.

3. Recapitulation of Experience

In outlining the basic themes, according to Hos. 11, mention has been made of Israel's history repeating itself. Israel will have to "go back to Egypt"; there, in another land of bondage, she must repeat the experience of oppression and suffering. However, as the previous bondage was but a preface to exodus and liberation, so the coming exile will lead into salvation. It would therefore appear that the literary recapitulation referred to above was in some sense a reflection of a pattern in God's working. The recurrence of the bondage/exodus theme (death/life, Cross/Resurrection) in Israel's history is emphasized by its having a counterpart in the way the themes reoccur in the written record.

4. The Art Gallery

We are not done with recapitulation. At point 2 above we have seen how the basic themes frequently reappear almost totally. The skeleton remains unchanged even if the accompanying "flesh" and "dress" alter. In other words, there is recapitulation of the whole story of Israel's rise and fall and rise again, with variations in detail, but on the whole there is not too much detail in these passages. But then there are passages showing considerable detail, especially where the sins and punishment of Israel are described. Stealing a suggestion from Professor G. B. Caird in his commentary on Revelation, I would suggest that another view of the unity of Hosea is clarified and reinforced if we compare the book with the room in an art gallery in which we are shown panoramas of the same scene from different viewpoints. These are interspersed with other paintings which give us close-ups of some of the detail that of necessity is lacking in the broad canvas. Thus Hos. 11 is a panorama of Hosea's whole message, whereas 6:1-10 and 7:1-7 are detailed "paintings" which enlarge upon the nature of Israel's sins more briefly delineated in ch. 11:2.

5. The "Integrity" of Hosea

It is right to remember that the OT is not the NT, and that its individual books must not be read in any facile way as though they recorded postresurrection events. Although both Testaments equally belong to the Bible of the Christian Church, the OT centers round the old covenant, and except in latent and prophetic forms does not contain the new covenant. Does this then preclude a Christian interpretation of Hosea? And would such an interpretation deny the integrity of the OT? We are faced with a paradox. The OT is Christian Scripture by confession from the earliest times —in fact it was the only Scripture of the earliest Christians—and yet it is plainly pre-Christian.

The position taken in the following pages is that a "Christian" interpretation is not only legitimate, it is essential if we are to interpret Hosea as Christian Scripture in a Christian fashion. As the Christian sees it, it is Christ who integrates the OT. He is its integrity, and without him it disintegrates into types of ancient Semitic literature. But this biblical paradox is not unique. Other writings, even nonbiblical ones, possess an integrity dependent on something outside themselves. An historical work can claim integrity partly on the basis that it points back faithfully to events in the distant past and accords with them; or a forecast or prophecy may find integrity not in itself but in future events towards which it leans and from which it takes its meaning. With this understanding we shall not compromise this integrity of the book of Hosea by illuminating it at times with the Light of the World which lightens every person and lightens especially "his servants the prophets" in the OT.

A Canonical Work

My approach to the text and to the various pericopes within the book can be described by a phrase of Paul Ricoeur's—"the second naiveté." Not unaware of the techniques and priorities of the historical-critical approach, indeed in some ways building upon them, I nevertheless prefer other means and other criteria. There is the feeling, perhaps not wholly justified, that by using other criteria one has "come out at the other side" but all the wiser for having passed through.

Much of what I mean by "the second naiveté" is also covered by the word "canonical." Here I am using it to refer not so much to the process of canonization as to the end product of that process: the Scripture as we now have it, with the imprimatur of the Church (and the Holy Spirit?) upon it. This, of course, is not to deny the historical approach to the Scriptures; it is merely to give priority to a different period in that Scripture's history. Rather than absolutize some period in the distant past because it "gave us the original deposit" and then use the modern critical apparatus along with our imagination to isolate what belongs to that period, is it not more historical and certainly less hazardous to opt for the period when Israel (and later on the Church) said: "This, as it is, is the Word of God"? Of course the text of Hosea is not all "original" (whatever that term means), for it has grown and developed and been added to and reinterpreted. Yet we should ask ourselves whether the sperm or the fetus is of more value than the baby or the grown person, because these can lay claim to "originality."

One commentator on the book rejects some parts of it on the grounds of "unity and elegance" and removes the "Judah" references because they are clearly a later addition. Does he know, however, just how Hosea or the editor viewed "unity" or "elegance"? And if he does (which I very much doubt), is he certain that those concepts entered much into the thinking of the editor when he was compiling a book about death and life? This commentary therefore will make no claim to deal with the "authentic" parts and expunge the "inauthentic" parts of Hosea. Moreover, it will take very seriously the "Judah" references, because if our eighth-century "Hosea" was indeed still speaking to seventh-, sixth-, and fifth-century Judah, then there is even greater warrant for believing that he is speaking to us today. And that is what counts.

SECTION I
SETTING THE STAGE

CHAPTER ONE
Hosea 1:1–2:1

1:1 We are told the name of Hosea's father but nothing more about his background. Was the latter unknown, or did the author consider it unimportant? Perhaps the latter. The book is so dominated by the first words, "The word of the LORD," that the specific historical context is passed over rather lightly. The word of the LORD "comes" to Hosea in time, in history, but it is timeless in its application (it "endures forever"). It is a word for all seasons and for all sorts and conditions of people. Moreover, the verb and preposition *hayah el* ("become to") imply a movement, in this case, from God to mankind. Thus the book begins in a way which is typical of the OT as a whole. At its center is the coming of God through his word. This word inevitably "comes" in history because its hearers themselves live in history. It is therefore historical, but it is "historical" in its own way, not in ours. Such matters as date, precise context and descriptive details are secondary to the fact of God's coming and to the effect of that intervention not only in its own day but in succeeding generations, as the word spoken continued to claim Israel's obedience and to maintain the covenant relationship.

The word "came" to Hosea and appropriated him and all that he said and did. His history, like Israel's, was a history created by the word of God. He was the opposite of a self-made man. Consequently, this history which was fashioned by the word of God now becomes an expression of that word; the word that came to him is now writ large in Hosea's own "(hi)story." In a frail and minor way the word became flesh and dwelt among us in the domestic tragedy of Hosea and Gomer. Thus the "word" of v. 1 is not just the cause of what follows, to be identified with certain authentic oracles or the *ipsissima verba* of Hosea. Rather, it is both cause and effect thereof. All that flowed from the word which came to Hosea is now taken up into that word, and becomes part of it.

The word is now not just the word of command but also the response to that command. The word, in other words, is the entire fourteen chapters we are about to study.

Four Judean kings—Uzziah, Jotham, Ahaz, and Hezekiah—are listed, compared with only one king of Israel: Jeroboam II. What is more, these Judean kings are listed first, despite the fact that Hosea prophesied in the north, and despite the almost certainty that their names were added at a later date than Jeroboam's. The simplest explanation accords with some of what has just been said. The prophecies of Hosea were not limited to his own time, to that of Israel in the time of Jeroboam II and his immediate but un- named successors. They were more than a tract for the times. They had enduring value, and this is emphasized by the mention of the Judean kings. That then is why they are given priority. Hosea, prophet to the north, in later generations was read in the south, perhaps with greater attention and respect than he ever received in the north, for Judah carefully preserved this foreigner's teaching as the word of God for their own day.

Much later again, the Church heard the book of Hosea as the word of God and added its own seal to the earlier stamp of canonization accorded by the rabbis. Consequently in our task now of trying to hear what the book of Hosea is saying to the present day, we find encouragement in our search from this very first verse.

THE IMITATION OF GOD: THE GREAT THEME STATED
(1:2–2:1)

Some commentaries on Hosea separate this section into 1:2-9 and 1:10–2:1 on the grounds that these were supposedly separate oracles. Further, some translations of Hosea not only distinguish the two oracles but remove 1:10–2:1 from its present setting and relocate it after 3:5. That they were originally separate oracles I do not dispute; neither do I deny that rearranging the text makes good sense. The question, however, is whether separating the oracles makes the best sense in this kind of commentary. I prefer to retain the existing order and treat 1:2–2:1 as a unity. The reasons are hinted at in the heading of this section as well as in the Introduc- tion, but more argument is necessary. In the Introduction reference is made to the recapitulation of central themes throughout the book, and also special mention is made of ch. 11, which can be taken as the classic statement of these themes. Indeed, B. Davie Napier ("Prophet, Prophetism," *IDB* 3:896-919) understands ch. 11 not only as central to Hosea but as expressing "the content of faith of classical prophetism." For Napier five themes can be identified here: "'Out of Egypt I called my son': Election and Covenant"; "'They went from me': Rebellion"; "'They shall return to Egypt': Judgment"; "'How can I give you up?': Compassion"; "'I will return them to their homes': Redemption." James M. Ward speaks of "the pattern that dominates the Book of Hosea" (*Hosea: A Theological Commentary,* p. 27), though he understands it somewhat differently.

The pattern, no matter how one defines it, is not a new one. Nor is it unique to Hosea, though it certainly manifests itself in Hosea in a remarkable and perhaps unique way. Let us examine the pattern a little more closely.

Besides the five themes that Napier finds in ch. 11, he identifies in Hosea two others which do not occur there. Prefacing the five themes noted above, he adds "'Thus says Yahweh': Word and Symbol" and concludes with another, "'A light to the nations': Consummation." Thus he produces seven prophetic themes in all. Such a pattern can be expanded, as is frequently done throughout the OT, or it can be pared down to essentials. The essentials would appear to be that within the assumed covenant mercies of God (which include creation, the election of Israel on behalf of creation, and the bestowing of God's gracious word) there lies a schema, that of rebellion by Israel leading first to judgment, then to redemption. It is this schema which dominates the whole book of Hosea; it can be found controlling its major divisions and in individual pericopes or chapters as well. It is as though hope always keeps breaking through. Dire warnings and promised destruction are followed by promises of restoration; fatal sicknesses carry hints of healing; chaos points to new creation; and despair points to hope. The sentence of death is rarely the last word, and the black cap so often donned becomes almost a sign of reprieve.

On theological, canonical, and perhaps literary-critical grounds, then, rather than for historical-critical reasons we shall regard 1:1–2:1 as a unity, as a variation on the great theme. The whole of ch. 1 divides into five subsections indicated by the paragraphs in the RSV translation; the fifth provides the longed for upbeat and is a kind of salvific coda.

1:2-3 Two of the greatest prophets, Moses and Jeremiah, tried to evade their vocation. Even Isaiah allowed himself the gentle protest "How long"? Hosea, on the other hand, faced with the unthinkable demand that he should marry a harlot, and with the unbelievable message that God has a wife, makes no protest. He marries a harlot and builds his testimony around something that looks surprisingly like the horror he was destined to oppose: Yahweh with a bride—sexuality in the Godhead!

What kind of harlot was this Gomer? Had she come from a brothel, or from a shrine where she served the cult? Or was she, like thousands of others, a "thoroughly modern miss" who had offered her virginity at a shrine because it was the fashion of the day? We cannot be certain of any one answer and must just rest satisfied that, whatever its nature, her harlotry was sufficiently apparent to symbolize "the harlot Israel." This appears to be the crucial issue, that Hosea's message was so clearly demonstrated that "all who run may read." Whatever she was to begin with, Gomer's later actions (like Israel's) left no doubt in the mind. She was a harlot, in name and in nature.

Many attempts have been made to justify God's strange command, to preserve God's moral reputation and to make things a little easier and more presentable for Hosea. The account of the marriage has been seen as allegory. "It didn't happen," say some, so "there is no problem." Or "the relationship has been romanticized." "Gomer was not a harlot but became one"; or "she was a harlot, but Hosea, like all true lovers, was blind and totally taken in by her." It has been common, and perhaps still is in some pulpits, to handle the book as a human love story, the story of a love that will not let Gomer go, so that from this his own bittersweet experience the prophet was led to learn of the greater love of God for Israel. The trouble is that this is not at all what is said in the Scripture. Incomprehensible and unpalatable as it sounds, this is the one marriage that was made in heaven. God commands Hosea to marry the harlot because God's word requires it and his will demands it.

These verses, then, describe the first of four events or "signs" in Hosea's life which must be set alongside certain others (some no less bizarre) that appear as symbolic acts in the lives of other prophets. Hebrew thought does not distinguish between the spoken word and resulting event as we do; in fact, the Hebrew

14

word *dabar* means at the same time both "word" and "event" (or 'thing'). Actions, for the Hebrews, do not necessarily speak louder than words, but sometimes they are the essential word which must be uttered in a certain context. Hosea the prophet had to "speak" in his marriage and in his children. His torn and sundered home was to be aligned with the family life of God. Hosea's family was to know and to reflect the awful anguish that God experienced because his "wives"—the land and Israel—had been faithless. Hosea must therefore share both the personality and the pathos of God. He must be smitten, stricken of God and afflicted, not that by his stripes others might be healed but that others might see and know.

1:4-6 This Asian book, the Bible, takes an Asian delight in the use of puns and plays upon words. Moreover, such delight can be deadly serious. In the Bible puns are not the lowest form of wit; frequently they are the means of conveying profound theology, and they may bear special vocational significance. Jeremiah's call includes a pun (Jer. 1:11-12). Another occurs in what may have been part of Amos's call (Amos 8:1-2). It is hardly surprising, then, that words are introduced at this early stage in Hosea which, with changing meanings in new contexts, not only weave in and out of the texture of this book but even become part of the pattern of all the rest of Scripture.

The burden of the prophet falls on his children. Like Isaiah's, the children of Hosea are living pulpits, walking placards (cf. Isa. 7:3; 8:1-4). The eldest son carries a loaded name which, in Erich Auerbach's phrase, is "fraught with [its] own biographical past" (*Mimesis: The Representation of Reality in Western Literature* [Princeton: Princeton University Press, 1953], 17). Later in the book more meaning will be heaped upon the name Jezreel; here it has at least two overtones. First, its pronunciation in the original is not unlike the word "Israel." It therefore was not inappropriate to use "bloody" Jezreel as a sign of the "end" of Israel. (Note that the pun in Amos' call was also used to signify the end of God's people.) Second, and far more important, Jezreel was a valley and a city which for Hosea and others of like mind signified blood shed in the nefarious interests of kingly power. The very word spoke of the oppressive abuse of such power, because it was there that Naboth the Jezreelite was done to death by Jezebel in violation of law, honor, and all human rights (1 Kgs. 21). Moreover, and this is in "the foreground of all the background," it was in Jezreel Valley that the dynasty represented by Jeroboam II, the Jehu dynasty, was established—and fearsome was the establishment thereof. Rarely has the principle that "those who take the sword shall perish by the sword" been better exemplified, for the dynasty that shed so much blood—including Naboth's—was itself destroyed in Jezreel by the warring zeal of Jehu. Behind the name of Hosea's eldest son lies all the horrors recounted in 2 Kgs. 9–10—a horror in no way alleviated because much of it was perpetrated as a result of prophecy and in the name of the LORD.

The principle of the ravening sword is proclaimed as still being operative, for the house of Jehu which was erected on violence and carnage is doomed to fall in like manner. The prophecy was fulfilled in 733 B.C. when Assyrian armies under Tiglath-pileser III subdued Galilee.

1:6-7 In the first sign (Hos. 1:2) it was the land that had been judged. In the second sign (v. 4) attention was directed towards the reigning dynasty, that of Jehu. Now in vv. 6-7 it is the house of Israel, the northern kingdom, that is condemned as the judgment continues and the indictment intensifies. This third sign is the naming of a second child, this time a daughter, who is destined to be known as "Not pitied." This time the word *lo* ("to him"), found with the earlier babies, is missing. Had Gomer consorted with another man? Thus, to the handicap of being a mere daughter there is now added the frightening stigma of a name that announces the idea that not even her father cares for her. But why a daughter? Was it merely that this child happened to be female, or is there more to it than such a simple fact of history? Is it not that femininity, even mother-love, seems to be "in the air"? The child of course symbolizes the bride of God and, further, the Hebrew word for "pity" derives from that very feminine organ, the womb. In this way then Israel's frailty and dependence are being stressed: the frailty and dependence of an infant girl or young bride. And then, in a fearsome way, the pity or love by which she should live is denied her.

But that pity is not denied to Judah. According to a later editor of our book—someone who is also to be regarded as a prophet—God is utterly free. The God who raised up a Jehu against the previous dynasty, then later judged Jehu's dynasty, is a God who is not limited. For Israel he speaks a word of judgment in their time; for

16

Judah in their time he speaks a word of continuing mercy, and mercy miraculously revealed, for v. 7 probably refers to the wondrous protection of Judah from the forces of Sennacherib in 701 B.C. Israel had been given both their mission and their punishment; Judah had theirs too, though the day of Judah's disaster was still to come. God is not partial, nor is he inconsistent; God both was, and is, the living God, and so he is abundantly unconstrained. The apparently "inconsistent" element in God is what has been called "contra-sistency": that which is apparently illogical and contrariwise, yet which hides that deeper unity of purpose which judges our seeming logic and our apparent unities. His "foolishness" that is wiser than human wisdom and his "injustice" which judges our virtue are qualities hidden in the eternal God.

1:8-9   A climax is now reached, a postponed climax (for weaning was delayed for almost three years in ancient Israel), but all the more climactic for the lapse of time. The fourth sign mentioned here takes us back to the roots of Israel's covenant relationship with God—then takes an axe to those same roots! The name of the third child, "Not my people," here introduces the language of the Covenant that appears first in Exod. 3:7, 10; 6:7, and then frequently throughout the OT and indeed on into the NT (cf. 1 Pet. 2:10). When he elected Israel God had designated them "My people." They are now his people and he is their God. He chose them, he liberated them from bondage, led them across the Red Sea, and at Sinai entered into the special relationship with them that is the underlying assumption and foundation of the whole of the OT. It is this relationship then, the hinge on which all else turns, that is now being repudiated. Israel, so long God's people, has now become "not my people." Moreover—and for good measure, in case the point is not clear—God adds "and I am not your God." This is emphatic enough in the English translation but is even more so in the original because the language is drawn from Exod. 3:14. There God reveals his name as "I AM WHO I AM" and then says to Moses "Say this to the people of Israel, 'I AM has sent me to you.'" What actually is said to Hosea is not "I am not your God" but "I am not your I AM."

This protracted "call" of Hosea has built up, as did those of Amos and Isaiah, to a declaration of divorce. Thus the old basis for Israel's existence, the grounds of their security and hope, have here been removed. Called out from among the nations in the days of Abraham, delivered from the nation Egypt and made to be God's "own possession" and "a kingdom of priests," Israel had rejected this special relationship and had made their way back among the nations. God's rejection of Israel was thus but a recognition and a confirmation of Israel's own choice. God's love, though endlessly patient, could not be coercive.

1:10–2:1 God's declaration of divorce links neatly with the divorce-court scene which begins in Hos. 2:2. Perhaps an earlier collection of Hosea's oracles omitted the intervening passage, 1:10–2:1 (2:1-3 in the Hebrew text). But I am taking our canonical version seriously; moreover, my canonical "obtuseness" has additional support. It comes from the dominant pattern of judgment/mercy, death/life, darkness/day referred to above and, as a corollary, a deepening conviction that the book in its present form came from the hand of an "evangelist." This person not only so ordered the book that it ends with the glorious gospel of ch. 14, but also began the book with three chapters where each ends in the manner in which the book as a whole ends, with promise and hope. The word that comes to us throughout the whole Bible moves *from* the heavens and the earth (which are pleasing to God), *through* sin and redemption, *to* a new heaven and a new earth from which sin and darkness have been banished. It has in its entirety this "U" pattern: from glory to glory via descent into the abyss. The pattern is to be found not only in the Bible as a whole but in many of its parts; the Servant Song of Isa. 52:13–53:12 illustrates it perfectly. Further, one is tempted to see behind and within all the "U's" of the OT the pattern of Jesus who descended, who emptied himself to die on a cross, and who now sits at the right hand of God and the Father. Are we not correct in seeing the NT good news foreshadowed in the "gospel" announcements made by these early chapters of Hosea? Can we not interpret these verses as pointing to a greater hope than their author ever imagined?

These verses may come from a "day of small things"; on the other hand they may have been spoken in the midst of some of the disasters promised in Hos. 1:2-9. All evidence of God's presence is absent from them, yet the words radiate joy and hope. They express a confidence so strong that they can describe what amounts to a great reversal of all that has been previously uttered. They look to a future relationship with God which goes beyond all Israel had even known, for Israel is to be more than just "my people"; they are to be "sons of the living God," enjoying an ideal unity under a "head" whom they have chosen for themselves rather than under a king whom they have merely inherited. Again the promise made to the patriarchs of Israel, that they shall be "like the sand of the sea," is to be fulfilled. This is more than just reversal or restoration. This utterance looks forward to the messianic age.

COMMENT

1. The word which God spoke to Hosea was new—shockingly new —radical, and unexpected. Like the other 8th cent. prophets it dealt with the end of the old covenant relationship, putting it in the harshest possible terms. The simplistic contrasting of Hosea's message of love with Amos's words of justice does not bear examination. There is nothing stronger or more unrelenting in all the prophets than some of Hosea's oracles.

The novelty of Hosea's utterances is hardly in dispute. What is less obvious is their very close dependence on the old traditions. Hosea is no creative genius, no revolutionary announcing a new ideology or a new morality. He blossoms on a stem that has old, old roots deep in the subsoil of Israel's history. In ch. 1 he draws on the Exodus traditions, on the history of the monarchy, and even on the theme of harlotry that had been introduced before (cf. Exod. 34:14-16). The extent of his indebtedness is well documented in Walter Brueggemann's *Tradition for Crisis: A Study in Hosea,* and we shall refer to this indebtedness in succeeding sections. Our present concern is to point out Hosea's dependence on the traditions and to suggest what this says to our own generation.

What we have in this prophecy, as in most of the other prophetic books, is a reinterpretation of old themes. The novelty is in the refashioning of primitive material, not in totally new beginnings.

Hosea is both conservative and radical, both continuous and discontinuous. He is a "back-to-the-Bible" preacher with sermons that shock the conservative and are too advanced for the liberal. His roots are traditional, his messages progressive. He begins with a *torah* which is nonnegotiable. This is his undoubted starting point, and whatever doubting or changing or interpreting he does is from this beginning and within the framework of this narrative.

His teaching shocks, frightens, repels, challenges, and destroys. But it points in radical ways to new horizons—even by faith to Christ; and it does this because it is rooted in the patriarchs, the Decalogue, and the whole saving history.

2. The churches of the Third World wrestle in mind and conscience with the problem of contextualization (or indigenization, or accommodation). How can the gospel of Jesus Christ be divested of its Western cultural swaddling clothes and be reclad in the cultures of Africa, Asia, and Latin America? What belongs to gospel and what is merely garment? What native cultural dress will distort the gospel and what will enhance it? Do some cultural features come trailing clouds so thick with idolatrous glory that they can only lead to syncretism? What can be borrowed and what must be rejected? Having first borrowed, then how is the infant borrowing to be baptized into the new faith? Where do the borrowings function in the new context and how do they function, if at all?

For many decades old Christendom has struggled with similar problems, but more in the language of "relevance" than contextualization. How can Christianity be more relevant for 20th cent. technological, urban mankind? True, for some in the West the questions have become opposite ones. Have we not been so concerned with relevance that we are left with little more than cultural trappings? Hasn't the faith been conformed to this world rather than being the agent of the world's transformation? Isn't the treasure wholly lost in the earthen vessel of a very earthly civilization? Or even more radically, wasn't our much vaunted Enlightenment merely the extension of the Dark Ages rather than their conclusion? Everywhere the Church agonizes over the issues of "Christ and culture."

Throughout this commentary we shall keep returning to this issue. In so many ways Hosea is our contemporary and has much to say. Let us then begin to hear.

DIVORCE AND
RECONCILIATION
Hosea 2:2-23

Judgment and punishment leading to restoration and blessing marks the pattern governing Hos. 1:2–2:1. A similar structure underlies the longer and more intricate passage in 2:2-23. Are there then other links between the two sections apart from such obvious ones as their common concern with the broken covenant and its renewal? Does ch. 1 provide the theological grounds for all that happens in ch. 2? Or is ch. 2 an explanation or theological elaboration of the pronouncements and events of its predecessors? Writers on Hosea seem to agree in using the expression "allegory" to describe ch. 2, assuming presumably that Hosea's historical marriage described in chs. 1 and 3 is allegorized and made to refer to the covenant marriage between Yahweh and faithless Israel. There is value in such usage of the text, but it is preferable to see the present passage as a further statement of the central truths which the book exists to affirm. Hosea is a book of many "sermons," all based upon a single if flexible text.

Where then was this particular "sermon" preached? Can we say, as some do, that it was delivered in a solemn assembly when the people of Israel gathered to renew the covenant with the LORD which they had so flagrantly violated? The thought fascinates but can be neither affirmed nor denied. What can be affirmed, however, is that wherever the oration first appeared, the imagined setting—and the one which provides some of its structure and vocabulary—is the city gate or "law court." A trial is in process, for someone has initiated divorce proceedings, and the speeches are what one would expect as the case is heard. There are accusations; there is pleading, indictment, threatened punishment, even a feeble defense (2:5). But what defense has faithless Israel? The verdict is not in doubt. Israel is guilty—horribly, inexcusably guilty—and so must pay the penalty. The details of the sentence rain down from

21

the Judge on hapless Israel (vv. 6, 9-13). Yet the execution is stayed and the impossible happens once again. Once more the clouds so much dreaded have proved to be big with mercy. The marriage which had irretrievably broken down is on its way to becoming a second honeymoon; and this time there can be no failure, for it owes nothing to Israel and everything to God (vv. 19, 20).

Several types of prophetic speech occur in the passage, and it is possible that the parts did not always add up to the same whole. Nevertheless, although it may not be "ab-original," there is a very clear theological unity present in the section. The way I have chosen to expound it is to take seriously the three "Therefores" (vv. 6, 9, 14). These introduce subsections 2, 3, and 4. The first sub-section consists of the original indictment in vv. 2-5.

2:2-5 Perhaps v. 1 provided the transfer from Hosea's children to the children of Israel, for clearly we have moved from the particular harlotry spoken of in ch. 1 to the national harlotry. At this point (2:2) the "children" are associated with the father and are commanded to give evidence. Later they will have changed sides and become identified with Israel in her sinfulness (vv. 4-5). The RSV translates *rib be-* as "plead with." Equally possible are such renderings as "denounce" and "accuse," because the word refers to the whole procedure before the court, and this naturally includes many kinds of utterances. Whether one leans to the RSV translation or to the others may depend in part on who we consider has initiated the divorce proceedings. Is it the wife or is it the husband? Opinions vary. If the wife is seen to be seeking the divorce on the grounds of her adultery, then the children can be understood as pleading with her to think again. Their responsibility then is not to secure a verdict against their mother but to help change her mind. In this case the process which leads to eventual acquittal and the second honeymoon begins in v. 2. The whole passage can then be seen as a plea for repentance, renewal, and restoration. On the other hand, if it was the husband who took the first steps to rid himself of his faithless wife, then the evidence of the children and the events leading to the joyous conclusion at the end of the chapter appear in a different light.

But which party did seek the divorce? Was it the mother or the father? The text may be read in both ways so that one is tempted to ask whether it is not correct to say that it is a case of "both and"

and not "either or." In both Hosea's and Yahweh's marriage the
bride was clearly the guilty party. It was her choice of other lovers
that brought about the breakdown, and her persistent faithlessness
was tantamount to suing for divorce. The passage can so be read.
At the same time the husband repudiates her in v. 2, and other passages regard her as no longer his responsibility. Further, this dual
seeking for divorce can be paralleled with a comparable theme in
the prophets, though it appears most clearly in Hosea; it is that because Israel has chosen no longer to be the "peculiar people" and
has opted to become like the nations, God will therefore cast her
off and send her back among the nations (8:8, 11, 13; 9:1-3;
Amos 9:7). The wish for divorce, therefore, at one stage at least
appears to be mutual, although it originates with the wife.

Hosea's determination to destroy the Canaanite mythology
from the inside allows him to draw his imagery largely from the
sensual mythology of Canaan. The trademarks of the tart are to be
exchanged for the nakedness which produces only shame, since
such is the sign of a "cast-off." And she is not only to be repudiated;
she is to be punished—with wilderness, parched land, and thirst.
Has love then become hatred, or is this the working of objective
justice, or is God of two minds on this issue (Hos. 11:8-9), or are
we in the presence of educative suffering? All these possibilities
have a measure of truth except the first, but the context of the
whole book directs us particularly to the fourth possibility. In
Hosea all things but sin may point to a final hopefulness; even
death, perhaps *particularly* "death," points to life.

The mention of wilderness (2:3) in a punitive context contrasts
with the wilderness of v. 14, which is its opposite: gracious and re-
storative. Is this paradox then an inconsistency, or what is it? Our
poet is not a logician; the Hebrew poet did not visualize his
"visual" images. He did not conjure up a picture that lingered in
the mind to produce conflict with the next image envisioned and
which in a Western context would have produced cries of "mixed
metaphors." His images were thought tokens serving different
masters in different contexts. Water could be both life-giving or
chaos-producing; the sword could stand for justice or mayhem.
Once used the token was thrown away; nothing remained but the
meaning intended, leaving no picture lightly or deeply engraved
that might resist invasion. The mind and heart were ready for the
next impressions to be received without prejudice. Throughout

Scripture—not only in Hosea—the concept of "wilderness" is of uncertain meaning. It is there the devil tempts; it is there that John the Baptist trains and Jesus prays.

In vv. 4 and 5 the children are now the children of Israel, and their mother's sin is identified with their sin. And in v. 5c, d, e their sin is described:

> For she said, "I will go after my lovers,
>   who give me my bread and my water,
>   my wool and my flax, my oil and my drink."

This sentence, along with vv. 8, 9, 11-13 which provide further elaboration, is the heart of the indictment and reveals a state of sinful alienation so deep and comprehensive that the rising note of horror in Hosea's voice becomes understandable. In Israel's state of rebellion as depicted here all the great biblical sins are comprehended and all the virtues excluded. Here are lust, apostasy, disobedience, errors of mind, distorted emotions, perverted instincts. Here are harlotry of body, mind, and soul. Here are materialism, idolatry, faithlessness, thanklessness—a life wholly and totally misdirected and willfully disoriented. Excluded from Israel's life are all the virtues that God speaks of in vv. 19-20: righteousness, justice, steadfast love, mercy, faithfulness, and knowledge of the LORD. The vignette of the prostitute who does not just stand and solicit, but who actively pursues her lovers omits nothing. Before the sin of the crucifixion there is no more full and fearsome description of mankind's turning away from God than this.

The evils and errors envisioned are not only moral, mental, emotional, political, and religious; there is a deep theological falsity hinted at which is to occupy the writer later in the chapter. In ch. 1 the harlotry protested against belongs largely within the doctrine of redemption. Israel is castigated because she has rebelled against the God of the Covenant, the God who has revealed himself in her history and has continued to be active redemptively in that history. The errors in the present chapter also begin in the context of the Covenant (i.e., within "redemption"), but in v. 5 we have clearly entered into the area of "creation." Israel's apostasy is now closely linked with creation and the promise of nature, and her breaking of God's covenant of salvation is tied to the simple but disastrous fact that she does not know who is in charge of the heavens and the earth. Beginning where all knowledge of God must begin, in his saving revelation, Hosea has now moved to the almost inevitable corollary of his created order. This is the beginning of a wonderful interweaving of the two "works" of God: the covenants with creation (Gen. 9:8-17) and the covenants with those chosen on behalf of creation (Exod. 19:1-5). In Hosea, when one of these covenants is found the other is not far away, and particularly is this so in the present chapter; for in it the author provides for these covenants a theological "minuet" which can lead us out of our contemporary harlotries and provide us with sure guides for our mission as the Church.

2:6-8   Following the indictment comes the first of the three "therefores." The word "therefore" is less common in Hosea than it is in some other prophets, where it often precedes the threat of punishment once guilt has been established. This is how it functions in vv. 6 and 9, for God's pronouncements must certainly be seen as promising punishment even though the punishment points to a happier outcome. Israel is to be severely restricted; hedges, walls, and other limitations will imprison her. Her frantic, obsessive religiosity with all its attendant dangers is to be given no opportunity to find satisfaction. Against her will she will be compelled to live prudently and soberly.

The punishment is not just vindictive or restrictive; it is designed to reeducate and reform. A change of heart intended is similar to that of the Prodigal Son in the NT. Suffering brings awareness and regret, if not remorse and penitence. George MacDonald once said "God is easy to please but hard to satisfy." Here in one of the most poignant sections of Scripture God reveals his loving anguish and is prepared to be easily pleased. Committed to giving mankind total freedom in the quest for disinterested love and obedience, God is sometimes prepared to compromise. The longing for the beloved is so great that he will even coerce. He removes the freedom she has to sin. Moreover, we are told indirectly that we need not always and completely carry the burden of freedom, that there are times when the "contra-sistency" of God permits us to pray "Take away this freedom; overwhelm me with your will; lower your ideals, and settle for something far less than my best."

In v. 7 God settles for a terrible second best. Unable to reach the lovers she really "loves," Israel finally in exasperation and frustration, not in love but peevishly and petulantly, pouts that any "husband" is better than none—even the old one. This outcome God is prepared to accept, and the loving misery that moves him to such acceptance shows in the pathos of v. 8. For the offerings in gratitude made to Baal actually came from God's dowry to Israel!

2:9-13   As thoughts of God's gifts lead into the first "therefore" of v. 6, so does remembrance of them in v. 8 provoke the second "therefore" and yet more restrictive punishment. Verse 8 begins with a suggestion of poetic justice, since the punishment is made to fit the crime as it so frequently does in the OT. Inability to recognize the source of life's necessities would be rewarded by their loss. Breaking covenant with the God of redemption would be followed by loss of his creation mercies. And this in turn would lead back to the first covenant and to God's refusal to continue the blessings of field and flock. This would result in Israel's being made stark naked and therefore exposed as in a livestock shearing, discarded and unwanted. At this point too, God would be revealed in his irresistible power. For that was the moment when he would be no longer the incognito God, hidden in creation and in Israel's history; he would be seen as he truly is. And if God's hand be against, whose shall be for?

The withdrawal of God's gifts would not only demonstrate Israel's separation from her true husband; it would make impossible all means of liaison with her pseudohusbands. The fervent cult which was directed towards the Baals could only continue if fueled with wine, beasts for sacrifice, and all manner of food for feasts. Gone was the time when God was willing to donate the means for his own cuckolding. He was patient and caring and longsuffering and merciful; but even loving deity has its limits, and those limits are reached when the faithless one utters "the abomination of desolation": "'These are my hire, which my lovers have given me'" (v. 12).

Not content with involvement in every kind of harlotry, with self-abasement at the shrines, with boasting about her prostitute's pay, and with breaking God's law (the Torah) by offering such wages in worship, Israel commits the ultimate sin of confusing God's gracious giving with what she has earned in a brothel. No wonder the intensity of God's indignation and punishment mounts to a crescendo of destruction, but still to end with the heartrending cry of the heart, "and [she] went after her lovers, and forgot me, says the LORD."

In English the clue to what is meant by "forget" is its opposite, "remember." The same is true in Hebrew: to "forget" is "not to remember" or "not to know," but (and the but is a considerable one) "remember" and "know" do not mean what we mean by them. For us they are largely activities of the mind, although they may on occasion indicate more. If I forget your birthday, it may indicate that "I don't think much about you." In Hebrew "remembering" and "knowing" are life commitments. They describe activities, a movement—from an attitude, a disposition, a judgment—to action, to a behavior pattern. "To know" (this is very important when studying Hosea) is the same verb as "to have sex with," that is, to relate to another not only with the mind but with the whole person: to identify with, to become at one with. When Hosea speaks of Israel's forgetting Yahweh in v. 13, the meaning is not far removed from divorce or apostasy.

2:14-23   The crescendo of accusation and of threatened punishment prepares us for the third "therefore," but when it comes we are equally unprepared for what follows. Two previous "therefores" succeeded by two announcements of punishment have built up into an expectation of further promised punishments. The rhetorical device is effective. But as we proceed, expectations are shattered and in stunned silence we listen incredulously to what is said; for the "therefore" opens, not into diatribe and disaster, but into grace abounding. This grace is grace alone, wholly unconditional, so that whatever change takes place in Israel is the result of God's grace and is not its prerequisite. The change is in fact in God, and it is indeed startling! It is true that the threats of punishment in previous verses had had overtones of re-education and hoped for reformation, and of course there is the same pattern of reversal in ch. 1. Nevertheless when we hear the words "I will allure . . ." in v. 14 we are expected to be wholly unprepared for what follows. We have been prepared to be unprepared, prepared by the "therefores," prepared by the incessant "I will, I will" (vv. 4, 6, 9, 10, 11, 12, 13), where each time the "I will" is followed by threats of disaster. Now in v. 14, after the third "therefore," comes the expected future tense, only this time it is a future about life and not of death.

But, as before, the punishment has been wholly of God's deciding, since the reconciliation and restored covenant depend entirely upon the will and character of God.

Verses 14 and 15 describe what God will do to make the new covenants possible. First he will allure, he will bring, he will speak, and he will give. Just as there were four promises made to Abraham, so there are four here to his successors. And what remarkable promises they are. They include the promise of land (v. 15) which is the same as one made to Abraham, but the others belong to the language of love. The "woman" that God will allure is someone who has proved abundantly that she cannot say "no." God's "seduction" of Israel will not be too difficult once Israel reaches the wilderness and escapes the agricultural environment that has caused all the trouble. The "back to Egypt" theme in Hosea (11:5) has this parallel theme of "back to the wilderness" and so to the delights of courtship with its splendors and new hopes of new beginnings.

The valley of Achor (Josh. 7:24, 26), with its memories of Achan and the painful reminder of the centuries of disobedience that followed the first passage through it, was the very opposite of a symbol of hope. This, however, was not going to defeat the God who can redeem all things and who even then could "see" the Cross, symbol of death and the world's hope. Geography, history, corrupted cultures, age, disillusion, habits of mind, and countless failures; despair, unfaithfulness, harlotry, apostasy, idolatry—none of these (or any other creature) is beyond the power of God to redeem when he is intent on renewal. So inevitably we read "she shall answer as in the days of her youth." And of course her answer had then been "I will."

Some of the details of the new marriage, or new covenants, are given in Hos. 2:16-23. The verses in their present form, whatever their origin, possess a unity which derives from their loving, saving content and concern with the restored covenants. Millennia before Julian of Norwich flourished in medieval England they announce "all things shall be well; all manner of things shall be well." This unity is even more apparent when the verses are seen in relation to vv. 2-13. The correspondence between threat and salvation, curse and blessing is quite remarkable. Point by point, as Walter Brueggemann has shown (*Tradition and Crisis*, 115ff.), the latter half of the chapter inverts the first half. The curse is removed brick by brick and a new house of blessing built in its place. Brueggemann thus begins a ten-point elaboration of the correspondence:

> (a) Verses 16-17 are concerned with the Yahweh-Baal conflict which clearly is at the center of the preceding trial scene. (b) Whereas Yahweh is forgotten in verse 13, in verse 17 it is Baal who will no longer be remembered. (c) In verse 2, Israel is compelled to remove her harlotry, while in verse 17 Yahweh will remove the cause of harlotry. . . .

A further way of regarding the unity of vv. 16-23 is to see them as describing "that day." The expression occurs three times (vv. 16, 18, 21) and points wholly to a day of victory and salvation. Gone are the ambiguities and clear elements of threat which we find in Amos or in Hos. 1:5. In ch. 2 it is wholly a day of salvation and new beginnings of which we hear. The change of appellation from "Baal" to "husband" is more than merely removing "the names of the Baals from her mouth, and they shall be mentioned by name no more" (v. 17). Hebrew *ish* ("husband"), with its corresponding *ishah* ("wife"), seems to speak of an endearing mutuality, a truly personal relationship, rather than the connection implied in the word *baal* with its suggestion of "boss" along with the sexual implications deriving from its possible original meaning of "fructifier."

Israel with her virginity restored can be expected shyly and demurely to say "I will" at the new wedding ceremony (v. 15). Yet Israel's "I will" to God is wholly dependent on the reiterated "I will" of God. Israel has said "I will" so often; she is an expert at it, a professional in fact. She has said "I will" to all and sundry. What is being offered her is the opportunity to say "I will" with utter sincerity and singleness of heart to her true husband. But how can he believe her? Has he not learned his lesson and finally admitted his wife's total inability to keep her promise? The answer is that the lesson has indeed been learned. He is not deceived. He knows that Israel's "I will" is anchored in his own constant "willing." In vv. 2-13 there has been the succession of his punitive "I wills." These are now supplemented and completed by his far more significant promises. Israel cannot cleanse her own cult; to do so is beyond her capabilities. But God can. He will remove her deeply embedded devotion to pagan gods (v. 17). Israel cannot restore the relationship between mankind and nature, broken when Adam fell. But God can, and he wills to do so. Israel cannot rid herself of the dangers of war and provide for her own security. But God can and will (v. 18).

THE CONCLUSION OF THE MARRIAGE PROCESS

The heart of the solution and therefore the clue to the chapter is surely to be found in vv. 19-20. This is the end of the courtship and the wooing. This is the irrevocable, legal, and utterly binding part of the marriage process. There are four stages in it. First the vow "I will betroth you to me," repeated three times. The word "betroth" with its modern connotation of engagement is not adequate to convey the meaning of the original. There is nothing in the least bit tentative about this, and the finality of the vow is emphasized by the second stage, which is the use of a word (used only here in Hosea) to stress that the vow is "for ever." The third stage would be the final promise to the bride's father about the scale of the dowry; it would normally come at the end of a long process of assessment, calculation, and bargaining. The bride-price, which God agrees to, comes after centuries of assessment and the most realistic calculation possible. This Groom knows he can expect nothing from the bride. Realistically and honestly she is not asked to make any vows; we have retreated from the conditional covenant of Sinai to something more like the covenants with Abraham and David. Only the Groom promises, but what promises they are! Not only are they unconditional and anchored firmly in the unchanging nature of God, but they are weighted with some of the greatest themes in Scripture, themes that belong to the very essence of God. "Righteousness" is that response to the Covenant which preserves the covenant community healthy and intact. "Justice" is righteousness in its legal aspect when the laws are God's laws and rightly administered. "Steadfast love" is love that one has promised to another, covenanted love; it therefore contains the strength of duty and sensitivity of kindness. "Mercy" is the pity and piety that belong more to the mother than to the male (because the word derives from the noun for "womb"). And "faithfulness" is "lived-out truth," or "Amen" in action. This very unequal marriage match, one-sided to the point of lunacy, this unilateral declaration of fellowship, is nevertheless wholly secure with such vows and such a dowry.

The wedding service is finished, the longed for moment has arrived, and the Groom takes his bride. Finally we should note that there are sexual overtones in "and you shall know the LORD" (v. 20) which hint at the joys of the wedding night.

2:21-23 In the movement from vv. 16-17 to v. 18 we passed from redemption to re-creation, that is, from God's particular provision in the saving history of God with Israel to the general provision of order and adequacy in nature and history. In vv. 19-20 we were back with what was presumed to be a redemptive counterculture, though not for long: for vv. 21-22 return us once again to nature, but this time, nature with a difference. This is because God's work in creation is beginning to look somewhat like his work of redemption. The two covenants which represent the two "presences" of God in his world are usually maintained in a polarized relationship (see Claus Westermann, *Creation* [London: SPCK and Philadelphia: Fortress, 1974], 117); that is, they are distinguishable and distinct but almost inseparable. In vv. 21-22 the usually impartial, impersonal, indiscriminate, unconditional creation covenant is beginning to change. Normally God in nature is seen to be objective, unbiased, neutral—requiring no response, being no respecter of persons. (Did not his Son stress that the sun shines on the just and the unjust?) Now a "stranger" has crept in, in the word "answer." Surely this is the language of prayer, of salvation, but not of agriculture and natural law. Can it be that the polarity is breaking down? We have already noticed that coercion and necessity which we expect in nature has begun to invade God's redeeming work through his people Israel. Has the reverse invasion commenced? Is the impersonal realm of seedtime and harvest, summer and winter under siege from the personal? Are intercessions now abroad at planting time, and is there a "prayer particle" envisaged in the atoms of the heavens, earth, and grain? We shall examine some of the implications of these questions later; meanwhile, we must take a closer look at what is being said.

THE GOD OF THE GAPS

Most of the problems to be combated have already been made very clear in the earlier part of the chapter. God, we might say, had been pushed onto the margins of Israel's life. He was still being acknowledged and still feted on high days and holy days; but was it really he who was being worshipped, or was it some contextualized substitute, some Baalized, syncretized idol called Yahweh? Most likely such an estimate is not far wrong. Moreover, there was good reason for such misguided, misleading contextualization. The reason lay in the culture of Palestine. In 1 Kgs. 20:28 is recorded a Syrian taunt: "The LORD is a god of the hills but he is not a god of the valleys." No doubt the saying was preserved because it echoed what was believed, if not said, in Israel itself; for it echoed and encapsulated a deep dark doubt at the center of Israel's faith. Was the God whom they had met on a mountain and who had proved himself in the wilderness able to deal with the agricultural economy of Canaan? Put bluntly, "Could Yahweh cope?" "Was he a big enough God?" To these questions the majority, whether consciously or unconsciously, articulately or inarticulately, plainly answered, "No." So the marginalization continued, and the margins grew ever narrower. Or to use a contemporary theological phrase, Yahweh had become the God of the gaps, and the gaps had got ever smaller. As the cultural influence of the Canaanites increased, so Yahweh decreased.

The "decrease," as we have seen, affected the covenants of both creation and redemption. Hosea 2:21-23 attacks the decrease within the sphere of creation. Here it seems to be much more than a decrease; it is almost a disappearance. The Baals had preempted the whole process of reproduction and everything that went with it. Yahweh had become locked out of a closed system which had functioned before he and his people had arrived, and functioned very successfully. At least this was how it was seen by most of the Israelites who were being made to feel backward and inferior as well as inexperienced in the new economy. In agriculture the Baals were everywhere: in the dying seed, in the rain, in the new life, in the heavens that thundered and gave light for the growing of the crops. From top to bottom this appeared to be the empire of the Baals, and if there was any place left for God it certainly could not be in the processes of fertility and growth, which obviously got on very well without him.

YAHWEH AND THE NATURAL ORDER

Hosea's counterattack is a clear statement of how the agricultural process does in fact work. He outlines the system in hierarchical fashion. Above are the heavens, and below is the earth along with the sown seeds or plants. Also there are the unexpressed gifts which pass from the heavens to the earth to the seed, such as nourishment and moisture. This was understanding of a system which everyone accepted. The only areas of disagreement were: Who makes it all work? And how does it work? The second question has been partially dealt with above. Hosea says it works rather like prayer does. Of course, it is not ordinary prayer that he speaks of, because only men, women, and angels pray; but it is something like prayer. The whole system is not just a machine. The personal God who made a world for persons to flourish in has left room for a personal element, even in the great "impersonal" structures of earth, moon, sun, and stars. Thus this is a world in which men, women, and angels can pray with confidence, because seeds even are "praying" and the soil hears. Prayer, in fact, is all around us.

How it works is nevertheless a secondary question depending on the first question, "Who makes it all work?" On this all else depends. Hosea answers loudly and clearly: "Yahweh makes it work." He is at the apex of the system. It is he who answers the heavens and not the Baals. Moreover, he is not only at the top of the system; he sows on earth. He is at the bottom as well, and in between and throughout it also, because the system is his and he made it, and it works as he planned it to work. Hosea does not question that it is a closed system. This he accepts, but what he does not accept, and what he counters with every breath in his body, is the view that it is closed to God, that God is otiose and shut out from his own creation. The ones shut out, however, are the Baals.

RETURN TO THE COVENANT

After this excursion into the problems of nature and religion, we return to the covenant with Israel. (The discussion is almost trinitarian, for we seem to move backwards and forwards between the first two articles of the creed: from "Maker of heaven and earth" to "suffered under Pontius Pilate, was crucified dead and buried.") The transfer is made naturally by reintroducing the name "Jezreel" with yet further unpacking of its almost limitless potential. This time it is not so much Jezreel the place, or Jezreel the symbol of a bloody history, or Jezreel the child of Hosea that is meant.

Jezreel is now Israel, a people decimated and underpopulated, being promised great fertility, but promised it by means of an agricultural pun. The word means "God sows." What more is there to say? The whole reproductive system is God's, and it works by prayer which starts in the ground with the seed. But how does the seed get there in the first place? What if there should be no seed, or what if there be seed but no sower? "Fear not," says Hosea, "all is taken care of." "God sows." He sows seed, and he sows people. The creation and redemption structures are both his. All is provided and provided for; even the labor is God's.

So now we have come full circle, at least a full circle enclosed by Hos. 1 and 2. The name of the first child is followed by the name of the other two. And just as Jezreel is now not a sign of past evil but of future rejoicing, so the other two now speak not of a broken covenant but of reconciliation. These great gracious deeds of God merit only one response: "and he shall say, 'Thou art my God'" (2:23).

DAYS OF WAITING
Hosea 3:1-5

The interpretation of this chapter depends upon answers given to some prior questions which are concerned with the book as a whole. Some have been referred to already; some belong to the narrow range of notoriously difficult OT issues, which makes conclusive resolution impossible, and compressed treatment both difficult and hazardous.

First we must decide how ch. 3 relates to chs. 1 and 2 as well as to the rest of the book. Chapter 3 has great similarities to ch. 1. They both contain commands of God to Hosea the prophet, and the forms of the commands are likewise similar. Furthermore, in each case Hosea is told to cohabit with a harlot or an adulteress, and a parallel is drawn between this relationship and God's marriage to adulterous Israel. Of course there are differences as well as similarities. One such difference is that ch. 1 is written in the third person, presumably by an editor or compiler, while ch. 3 reaches us in the first person and therefore is Hosea's own account. Are we to regard chs. 1 and 3 as biographical accounts that are the starting point and basis for the whole prophecy, or are they less than biographical, so that the book is built on other foundations? Again, is ch. 1 a retelling in other words for other ears of the same experience that Hosea relates in ch. 3, or does ch. 3 merely take up where ch. 1 ends and so continue the tale by giving us the next installment in the drama?

I shall assume that both chs. 1 and 3 are rooted in history, and that God did command Hosea, and that things happened much as they are recorded. I would not use the word "biography" about either chapter, for if we should choose to do so, then we would be in error in regarding such "biography" as the book's foundation. Inasmuch as there is indeed biographical material present, I lean to the view that ch. 3 continues where ch. 1 ends. This continuity is significant because it resembles a similar continuity in God's relationship with Israel, though the "biographical" continuity is not the main link between chs. 1 and 3.

On the other hand, ch. 3 is a further statement of the great theme already described in ch. 1. It is another variation on the common theological schema, adding its own new insights and deepening what has gone before. The theological relationship with ch. 1 is more important than the historical. In ch. 2 we find, I believe, the real basis for chs. 1 and 3. This is because that chapter describes the God-Israel marriage which is the clue to the raison d'être of the Hosea-Gomer relationship.

The second set of questions follows naturally from the first. They concern Hosea's marriage and are particularly curious about the identity of the woman in ch. 3. I have already said that I consider ch. 3 continuous with ch. 1. This effectively rules out the theory that the happenings of 3:1-3 are to be identified with ch. 1 and that this is the original marriage as Hosea once told it. Yet the question remains open as to whether the woman of ch. 3 is Gomer or a second harlot. Certainty is impossible, but I assume the woman to be Gomer, because in the parallel marriage of God and Israel Israel remains the continuing factor. The introduction into Hosea's story of a second female makes little sense, though my interpretation of ch. 3 would not be greatly altered even if Hosea had taken a second wife. I regard the theological theme as more determinative of meaning than that the object of Hosea's affections should be another woman. The following discussion of the third problem should add further comment to my somewhat dogmatic stance adopted above.

The third problem is raised particularly by v. 5 with the reference to "David their king." Is this reference original? If so, does it convey the same message as do the southern references found in chs. 4–14? If 3:5 is by a later hand, then how late is it? Has the later hand not totally misunderstood the reference to "king" in v. 4 and assumed that Hosea was critical of the northern kings but supportive of the house of David? Is it not better to regard v. 5 as a later addition, thus excluding it from the original deposit and therefore expungable from our field of interest?

As explained above, however, I shall examine the book as we have it. So we will take seriously the Judah and David references and will also take very seriously the context of the original deposit inasfar as we can discover it. We do so because the word of the

LORD came to Hosea livingly, historically, shatteringly in his own time yet continued to speak and reverberate later on in Judah and in succeeding generations. We in our turn, therefore, are now trying to hear the original along with those reverberations. Hosea's words mean more to us simply because they meant much to Judah. Our listening today must hear Hosea the man but also Hosea as Judah heard him. For both we and Judah listen primarily not to Hosea but to the God who once started a conversation with Hosea and who has kept drawing others into that conversation ever since.

God's conversations in the Bible are like this. They go on and on, which no doubt is part of what is meant when it is said that the word of the LORD endureth forever. One thing about these enduring conversations must be emphasized because it is pertinent to what we are about. A conversation which begins with very specific roots in an historical context can never wholly break loose from that context or deny its importance as a *sine qua non* of all that follows, because it was that which gave it birth. Nevertheless, the further the conversation moves into the future, the more it will acquire metaphorical, symbolic, theological overtones. Built upon the particular, it inevitably becomes more general; founded upon concrete facts and events, it later must widen in ways which can include the needs of later generations and other contexts. This it does, not by a complete uprooting but by a metaphorical and theological flowering which continues to be nourished by the original historical soil. Roots, flower, and fruit are a unity, and faithful comment treats them as such.

3:1-2   The form of these verses is identical with Hos. 1:2-3 and similar in some respects to 1:4-5, 6-7, 8-9. There is the command of God to take a woman, the reason for the command linking it to God's love for Israel and, finally, the execution of what has been commanded.

The command is unclear if we ask mere biographical questions, such as where does the word "again" belong? Is it where it is placed in the RSV, or does it mean "the LORD said to me (again)"? Or should it even be translated by "again" at all? Perhaps it means "Go and love another woman" or even "Go and make love once again to your wife." Both translations are permissible; perhaps it is even preferable to have both. No doubt the precise meaning was most important to Hosea, but need it be so to us?

What is quite certain in 3:1 is that the same Hebrew root for "love" is used four times. This is the earliest reference in the OT to the love of God; moreover, the love that is called for from Hosea is a reflection of the love God has for Israel. In fact God's love dominates the chapter. Therefore this chapter must be given a prominent place in the understanding of the whole book. The themes of election, rebellion, punishment, compassion, and redemption we find elsewhere; but in ch. 3, as in ch. 2, these themes conclude with the faithful response of the beloved. Even ch. 11 does not include such a response from Israel (Ephraim), only from the people of the South. Yet its links with ch. 2 are particularly close. It is as though the same message were merely being translated into another medium, in this case from the allegorical/theological into the historical/personal. Hosea now has to dramatize on the stage of his own home all that has been threatened and promised in the previous chapter.

The woman is shown as unloving but not wholly unlovable, for her paramour (or friend) still loves her. The failure in relationships is a failure of faith and constancy. In Israel's case this means she is attracted to other gods and to their cults as symbolized by the cakes used in the ritual of the worship of Baal. The same indiscriminate and trivializing use of the word "love" is found in v. 1 as is so painfully common in our usage today. The word is used for both marriage and adultery, to describe both God's love and a passion for Canaanite cakes! God's love is thus made to compete with cookies —and the cookies win.

Hosea, obedient as always, buys the woman. The writer, who leaves us in the dark about her identity, gives us details of the bill. Why the price should be important while her name is not escapes the modern reader, and we can be worried that we do not know the answer; but such details in Scripture are rarely irrelevant. Does the verb "buy" show she was a slave, or does it prove Hosea was short of cash? We do not know. The point at least is that there was a price (for she was redeemed), and after the price was paid she belonged to Hosea—ransomed, restored, and forgiven, but not yet healed. That would come later.

The parallelism of v. 1 is repeated in vv. 3 and 4. What Hosea does with the woman is a prophecy of what God will do with Israel. These two verses and their contents also parallel those parts of ch. 2 where God declares he will withdraw some of his gifts as an educative punishment (2:3, 6-7, 9, 12). Hosea now orders a form of house arrest which will keep her out of temptation's way. Virtue will have to be forced upon her. No sexual relationships will be permitted her, not even with Hosea. If she is to be denied intimacy, then he will share with her in the deprivation. Their relationship must be mutual, because this is deprivation with a purpose, the purpose mentioned at 2:7. The two husbands (Hosea/God) are each seeking a change of heart in their beloved.

The deprivation described in 3:3 is to be mutual for a second reason. The relationship described is a sign of the greater relationship between God and Israel. At that time it existed only in a formal sense—having the form of marriage but not its content. Verse 3 describes a relationship where the financial and legal aspects are complete; the woman has been bought, she is resident with him, she is now his possession, is under his authority, and is kept away from all other men. The shell of marriage is there indeed but not the essence, which is love along with its physical manifestation. The form awaits the content, and that in turn awaits the loving response of the woman. The kept woman must first become a loving bride.

If v. 3 points to the happenings of v. 4, it is the latter verse alongside v. 5 that explains v. 3. Verse 4 describes Israel's deprivation, but it is deprivation within the covenant. The form of the relationship is there because God so wills it, but the essential relationship is absent and will remain absent until Israel can learn to love. Israel's deprivation consists of the loss of six things, listed in pairs. These are king and prince, sacrifice and pillar, ephod and teraphim. The king and prince signify the political realm, so that this announcement leaves us in no doubt that God's writ still runs in the sphere of government. The other two pairs belong in the arena of the cult but may point to different aspects of it. Sacrifices at the shrines where the pillars stood were designed to provide forgiveness of sins, and so of events in the past. Ephod and teraphim are perhaps to be seen as ways of learning God's will for the future. Thus Israel is to be deprived in the secular and spiritual areas of life, and to be robbed of assurance about both past and future. But are those six things that are to be removed beneficial to Israel, or is Israel better off without them? Are the people being deprived of life's blessings, or are they being taught to say "goodbye" to some of the temptations which had led them astray? The answer is clearly "both." Used properly the six items were among God's gifts intended to keep life within the covenant whole and healthy. They helped put flesh and blood on the covenant skeleton; they were part of the means for securing the "knowledge of God," a term we have already noted bears sexual overtones. They were means and opportunity, being part of the marriage bed that God gave to his bride. But the bed had been defiled, and that which was created to join husband and wife had done just the opposite. Kings and princes had led Israel to autonomy and independence of God, and the cult had been used to serve idols. Israel's religion had then become unfaith. The good gifts of God had become corrupted and in consequence had to be removed. One day, when these gifts should once more lead to the knowledge of God rather than to the knowledge of idols, they might be restored.

The days of waiting will end, and then the reason for the waiting and the nature of the waiting will become clearer. The word "afterward" in v. 5, therefore, introduces a great turning point, for here is the longed for climax. That climax centers on three verbs: "return," "seek," "come in fear." It is the climax of Israel's response and corresponds in part to 1:11 and to the last phrase of 2:23. Whether the deprivation described in 3:3 ever brought a change of heart in "Gomer" we are not told, so no matter what its significance was to Hosea it cannot be—and perhaps is not meant to be—important to us. The importance lies in Israel's return, and seeking, and coming in fear; yet even more, its importance lies in God's planning for her conversion and then in his waiting for it to take place. Having heard then that God has decided to preserve the covenant, one then asks "Why?" And "What does God do meanwhile?" The answer is clear. He loves, and the love is a lover's love. It can plan, and can will, and can act, but ultimately it can only wait, only live in hope of the "afterward." It is the love of the lover Christ who stands at the door and knocks, and who then just waits (Rev. 3:20; cf. Cant. 5:2-8).

It may be that Hos. 3:5 was not in Hosea's original draft, but it is there in our Bible, transmitted by the communities of faith— Israel and the Church—with no suggestion that it was extraneous or distorting, or even of second rank. How then does Hosea's hope which budded in Judah blossom today? The verse, as we have noted, follows the general pattern of Hosea's *kerygma*, but the preaching is never precisely the same. Each variation on the great theme brings its unique contribution, deepening the emboss here, adding shadow or a new turn there. What then does this verse add?

1. God waits, and the waiting is rewarded. God loves, and the love is not in vain. God is satisfied with nothing but a full response in conversion.

2. There is a place in the grace of God for both punishment and deprivation. People are not necessarily demeaned by intended suffering and discipline. Sometimes they are lifted out of the trough of human bitterness and vindictiveness when mercy and love are used to reform the lost and save the abandoned.

3. The conversion is shown to be total. As in 1:11 one must assume that all the children of Israel are here included.

The new-found communion with the covenant God has now restored the fellowship of all Israel. Together north and south shall return. The turning back to God is reflected also in the turning to the neighbor—and even to the brother, something which is much harder to do.

This return is therefore not a private, inward turning. It has social and political results; whole societies and countries are affected. The rehabilitation even extends to the much maligned cult because the word "seek" is a technical term which more often than not means seeking God at a shrine. If the "return"—with its overtones of confession, forgiveness, and reconciliation—corresponds to the "sacrifice and pillar" of v. 4, then the "seek" may reflect the "ephod and teraphim," for these belong in shrines and are used in seeking to know the will of God. The mention of "David their king" then completes this list of correspondences. The shrines and their apparatus had been set aside because they too were a hindrance, not a help. But the banning order was only for "many days"; it was not a total repudiation, only a time for amendment of life. Shrines and ritual, kings and governments have their use and are only condemned when abuse has replaced use. Such a "revised" v. 5 thus sees the "latter days" as the end to the "many days" of the original in vv. 3 and 4, when the gracious punishment will have done its work and all is restored and *shalom* reigns.

God's "goodness" in the last phrase presumably includes his gifts through nature as outlined in 2:8-9. With this the restoration is complete. Israel as a whole has wholeheartedly returned in faith to God. The cult has been restored and the monarchy reestablished and honored. The spiritual and the secular are once more locked into God's purposes. But is the great hazard, nature, finally disarmed and domesticated? In this new faith there is to be found a new reverence for Yahweh, one which no longer doubts his dominion over all things but which approaches the fruits of fertility in confidence and safety because they are known to belong to the LORD.

FURTHER COMMENT

1. The inner dialogues continue; in ch. 3 they are added to and continued by the later "improvement" made in the southern kingdom. Without the reference to David in v. 5 a strong case could have been made that the book of Hosea is opposed to monarchy per se. It may be that Hosea himself was so opposed, yet it was not the prophet who has been canonized but the book which bears his name. The book as we have it does have a place for monarchy, even the Davidic monarchy. So also does the NT which exists to exalt the Son of David.

The monarchy dialogue is therefore furthered in this chapter. Much else is furthered too. Does Hosea—and do the prophets—condemn sacrifice utterly? This chapter makes sober comment on both the dangers and the values of sacrifice and of the cult in general. There is here a cautious "yes" and "no" to ritual, depending on whether it remains a servant or has turned traitor.

2. The place of punishment, discipline, and the general use of power to restrict and deprive are matters never far from much modern conversation. Chapter 3 contains a positive affirmation of their value. They are declared to work as long as they are set in a nonauthoritarian context, one in which love is seeking to find a way and where the agony of the depriver is greater than that of the deprived.

3. The insistent theme of judgment/salvation begins to have a strange effect on the student of Hosea. One becomes not only accustomed to the theme, but one expects to find it and feels disappointed if sometimes it is not there. I have come to think of it as the "plagues syndrome" and to characterize it as "bad news is good news." (These expressions already take us beyond Hosea, but let us stay with him for the time being.) In three chapters we have already encountered the phenomenon several times, and there is still much

more of it to come in later chapters. Bloody battlefields spell hope, rejection becomes acceptance, repudiation becomes mercy, threats turn into promises, punishment brings love, and deprivation leads to faith. The tale seems endless: always the valley of the shadow leading to goodness and mercy and to dwelling in the house of the LORD.

Mention of the plagues and the Twenty-third Psalm have already hinted at a widening context, for mention of the plagues can refer as much to the book of Revelation as to Exodus. Hosea is a very clear example of this great unifying theme of Scripture and as such helps clarify the rest; in turn the prophet is interpreted best in the light of the other sixty-five books of the Bible. The bondage in Egypt, culminating in the plagues, leads to the sunburst of the Exodus, while the wilderness is the way to the Promised Land. On and on throughout the OT we travel the same road until it leads to the Cross and Resurrection which we can only fathom after we have trodden this same OT road (Luke 24:25-27, 44-46). Light from the rest shines from Hosea; light from the rest illumines Hosea. We learn to expect the disasters, to anticipate the loss of land, of freedom, monarchy, and the cult. This is because we learn that salvation is not an avoidance of these, a *deus ex machina* escape from horror, but is of a God loving within the horror. The horror has thus somehow been sanctified, taken up into the great plan, and become the harbinger of salvation. This then is more than a word from the LORD just for today; it is the word of the LORD for every day.

SECTION II
THE PRESENT STATE:
NO KNOWLEDGE OF GOD

THE CONTROVERSY AND THE REASONS FOR IT

Hosea 4:1-19

The first three chapters of Hosea, despite many problems, divide naturally into three sections all dealing with the two parallel marriages. Each of the three chapters moreover falls into Hosea's "theme pattern" of fall and rise. Beginning with ch. 4 there is now little that is either obvious or clear except the difficulty of discerning any order. Yet the flow of these eleven chapters is towards the great saving climax of ch. 14. This suggests, first, that the overall theme pattern has determined their final arrangement, and second, that there is in fact a unity waiting to be discovered. It is a unity however which consists of many fragments. These fragments may of course have been oral announcements or written productions or a combination of the two. What cannot be gainsaid is that they have come down to us in a literary form which has been carefully presented, and it is this form upon which we are called to comment. I propose to divide the text of chs. 4–14 into three sections. The first division (chs. 4–7) outlines the state of the nations. The second (chs. 8–11) rehearses the spiritual history of Israel, while the last (chs. 12–14) presents both retrospect and prospect.

It is tempting to try to fit these three divisions into the marriage pattern which rules chs. 1–3, but this would be more of an imposition than the one I have finally chosen. It centers on what Hosea calls "knowledge of God." This is a basic theme of the whole book, and is one that comprehends everything else that Hosea speaks about. Thus chs. 4–7 can be seen to describe Israel as living without this "knowledge of God," while chs. 8–11 revolve round the history in which this knowledge was revealed by God but spurned by Israel. Finally chs. 12–14 move towards what Hosea means by the "saving knowledge" of God.

4:1-3 These verses have several functions. First, they provide a link with chs. 1-3 by continuing the courtroom atmosphere of ch. 2. They even employ some of its vocabulary (cf. 2:19, 20). Second, they introduce a great new division of the book with the phrase "Hear the word of the LORD, O people of Israel"; and third, they summarize the case for the prosecution that is to be elaborated upon later. There seems to be little doubt that these verses exist both as a kind of summary of and as a heading for several succeeding chapters, rather than as being continuous with 4:4-7. They are addressed to all Israel, while the addressee in v. 4 is "the priest."

Israel is also addressed as the "inhabitants of the land," a phrase which reminds the hearer both of God's lordship of the land, asserted in ch. 2, and of Israel's abuse of the fruits of the land. The reasons for the controversy then follow, first negatively (4:1c, d) and then positively. Faithfulness and kindness, fruits of the Covenant, were absent, as was the knowledge of God which was the basis for the Covenant. In the original Hebrew the reference to 2:19, 20 is abundantly clear. Having cited Israel's sins of omission Hosea then lists the evils that are everywhere committed. He does so in language that is very close to that of the Ten Commandments.

Continuing then with his brief against Israel the writer follows the classical pattern, so clear in the Ten Commandments themselves, where the religious (i.e., the God/man relationship) has priority over the ethical (or man/man) relationship. If the virtues which distinguish life within the Covenant (namely, faithfulness, loyalty and knowledge of God) are lacking, then inevitably, as night follows day and as the last six Commandments follow the first four, there is to be found swearing, lying, killing, and so forth. For a society without moral norms ends in self-destruction.

The dependence of works upon faith is witnessed to everywhere in Scripture. This fact is widely if not universally recognized by modern readers of the Bible. More difficult to accept is the causal relationship implied in 4:3. Is it true that religious and moral disobedience result in the land mourning (or being wasted), and that even the beasts of the field, the birds of the air, and the fish of the sea are then taken away? But first a technical question. Does v. 3 continue the description of things as they are? In other words, is the RSV correct in translating by the present tense? Or should we read the verse in the future tense and so, instead of understanding it descriptively, take it as a sentence of punishment?

Overtones arising from the Flood narrative might incline one to read the verse as an announcement of judgment to follow; but no argument is conclusive, and our uncertainty in the matter is not important. This is because what is not in doubt is the cause of nature's mourning, namely God. Thus whether the disaster has already fallen or is yet to fall matters little from our point of view, which must be a theological one. What does matter is the inter-relationship of the religious, the moral, and what nowadays must be termed the ecological in any natural disaster. Hosea is saying that the earth is the LORD'S and the fullness thereof, but that the earth and its fullness are all of a piece with the life of the covenant people, because the covenant God has a covenant also with the earth in all its fullness (Gen. 8:8-10). Autonomy, either of mankind or of nature, is one of our modern myths. For some today it is even a datum or a virtue to speak in this way, but such has no support from Hosea or indeed from any part of the OT. Distinctions are indeed made, as in these verses, between the religious and the moral, between the latter two and the ecological, between saving history and profane history, between creation and redemption. But these distinctions do not invalidate the overall unity of the concept. In the view of the prophets there is a harmony in all things, an intertwining and interdependence. In fact it could not be otherwise because the Creator and Sustainer of all is himself One, and he has ordered his creation as one. It was the ancient Greek philosophers who separated between heaven and earth, the ideal and the actual, body and soul, matter and spirit and not the great Hebrew prophets. For the prophets the only separation God has made is between good and evil, symbolized by light and darkness (Gen. 1:3).

Our present age with its concern over the exploitation of natural resources and its care for the environment and for the preservation of existing species of beasts, birds, and fishes is well able to hear some of what Hosea is saying in Hos. 4:3. We know how human sin and greed go hand in hand with "taking away" (v. 3d) many of God's creatures. In fact, the link between morality and ecology we can forge with little difficulty. But part of the Church's mission is to announce that this link is dependent on the greater link: the link of faith in the covenant God. As in Gen. 3 the trouble begins in the religious realm, so that in consequence nature is made to suffer. Can the Church not learn to say once more what Hosea is saying here, that often it is not that people perish because nature strikes but that nature is stricken because people are perishing through disobedience?

4:4-10 Hosea now begins to "unpack" the general indictment made in Hos. 4:1-3, where the movement was from religion, through morality (both individual and social), to the natural environment. Where then does the main responsibility lie? Why is it that there is no faithfulness or loyalty or knowledge of God? Without hesitation Hosea points the accusing finger at the priest. If the fruits of the Covenant are missing, then the blame must be laid at the door of the Covenant-keeper par excellence, namely, the priest. Israel, the kingdom of priests (Exod. 19:6), can be priests to the world and to nature only if they themselves are properly priested. Unfortunately these keepers of the Covenant were following too closely in the footsteps of Aaron their "father" (Exod. 32). He had led Israel into idolatry rather than ensuring they remained faithful to the conditions of the Covenant.

Before we listen to what is being said in more detail we must look at the setting of this chapter and discover the identity or identities of those addressed. Who is the priest addressed here, and what are the circumstances surrounding the indictment? Is it one priest with his family who is under attack and one particular prophet (Hos. 4:5), is it a group of priests and prophets, or is it priesthood and prophecy in general? The argument that it is an individual priest is strengthened if we compare this chapter with Amos 7. The latter begins with three visions, all of which are statements of the prophet's message (Amos 7:1-9). These include threat, judgment and grace. Immediately following (Amos 7:10) a priest enters into controversy with the prophet and seeks to quiet him. Amos thereupon responds with judgment and threat against both the priest and his family. In Hos. 1–3, also, we have three statements of the prophet's message, and those too include threat, judgment, and grace. The threat and judgment then continue into 4:1-3; whereupon we have controversy with a priest. The latter is then quieted by the prophet before he proceeds to judge and threaten the priest and his family. These similarities argue that it is a single priest who is intimidated here, perhaps the chief priest, and this interpretation is even supported by mention of the priest's mother and children. Do we then assume that vv. 4-10 and perhaps the whole of vv. 4-19 center round the inadequacies of a particular priest at a particular shrine contemporary with Hosea? Francis I. Andersen and David Noel Freedman answer yes *(Hosea)*. My answer is more complicated and distinguishes between an original experience of Hosea and what the canonized version of his book was eventually made to say. I think the whole chapter may have had its origin in an experience in a shrine similar to the experience of Amos in Amos 7, but I do not believe that the final version can be limited merely to recording that experience; even less do I believe that a modern commentator should remain within these confines.

If we assume a particular priest for the original experience described here, then why was the particularity so muted? Why was there no name given or location mentioned or a clear placing of the incident in the historical process? One could ask similar questions about the whole of Hos. 4–14, because from beginning to end virtually all marks of a particular historical setting are absent. If one compares these chapters with Isa. 40–55, which are notorious for a like absence of historical anchorage, it must be admitted that Deutero-Isaiah at least has the Cyrus references (Isa. 44:28; 45:1). Hosea 4–14 possesses nothing comparable. Why is this so? Were the references later removed? If they were, then would this removal account for some of the irregularities in the present text? But why are the references not there? The obvious answer lies in the direction suggested by Brevard S. Childs. Assuming that a unique confrontation with a particular priest lies behind ch. 4, one has to assume in the light of the rest of the book that this priest was typical of the great majority of the priesthood. He was therefore from the beginning a type, a representative. The particular already represented the generality, and it was this that made him noteworthy and meriting record. As one swallow does not make a summer, neither does one debased priest mean that all priests were alike. Even in Hosea's mind it was the symbolic and the metaphorical quality of this priest that made him significant. His theologizing was present from the moment he remembered and recorded the event, if not from the very time of confrontation itself; and this symbolic, metaphorical, and theological factor continued to increase. Thus even as it increased, its historical anchorage grew ever less significant. It may be, as we have suggested, that the trappings of history were deliberately reduced in order to strengthen the theological value of Hosea's indictments, and this process could have begun very early. Then when these verses were speaking directly to Judah in a later century, still more of the marks of history might have been shed in order to release for all times and in all places a power and authority which might have been limited by too much stress on details of identity, date, and locality. We are looking then at a priest who was both "priest" and "parable" and whose parabolic force has grown and continues to grow even as the generations see their own priesthood reflected in him and learn from that reflection.

An outburst from the priest (which we must imagine) is immediately countered and stilled (v. 4). Blame lies not with the prophet Hosea but with the priesthood. They are in fact the guilty party; but the trouble is that when the priests sin then their contemporaries all sin with them: their colleagues at the shrine — the prophets, the nearest and dearest in their own family, and eventually the whole flock committed to their charge. Does such a heavy blame really rest upon their shoulders? Is not this condemnation and sentence of rejection more than they deserve? The answer is given very clearly in v. 6; God's people are destroyed for lack of knowledge. This has come about because the priests have rejected knowledge, and it is for this that they in their turn are being rejected.

The knowledge referred to is, of course, the knowledge of the LORD. This concept is central to Hosea's whole prophecy, and reference to it occurs at some of the most significant places in the book (2:20; 4:1; 6:6; 8:2; 13:4). Absence of this knowledge along with the lack of faithfulness and of loyalty form the religious root of the apostasy Hosea is attacking. We must therefore now examine two questions. First, what is meant by the knowledge of God, and second, what is the relationship between this knowledge and the priesthood?

1. Hans Walter Wolff quite categorically declares that Israel's relationship to the knowledge of God in Hosea corresponds "in every respect" to the NT believers' relationship to the gospel (*Hosea*, 93). This is not an overstatement. In the interests of brevity I shall summarize the main features of this "OT gospel."

a. The knowledge is a revealed knowledge as distinct from a knowledge based on speculation, myth, nature, cogitation, or mysticism and comes actually from the traditions of Israel, in particular from the tradition of the Exodus (13:4-5).

b. It is knowledge of God as the only God, and as such the saving and healing God (11:3; 13:4).

c. This knowledge is constitutive of the community of Israel because Israel has come into being through the Covenant, which in turn is founded on this knowledge. When the knowledge is present peace dwells in society and harmony in nature (2:16-20). When the knowledge is missing all community is lost and nature mourns its ruined state (4:3).

d. The knowledge comes to the individual through his or her life in the community, including both formal and informal education, and through participation in the rituals of the community where the ancient traditions are rehearsed and relived. It is also through life in the community and its cult that the knowledge is nourished and maintained.

e. The knowledge of God is far more than the awareness of facts or acceptance of dogma; behind the noun *da'at* lies a verbal stem that includes sexual intercourse in its range of meaning, as we noted earlier in connection with the marriage issue. Although there is little cause to look for sexual content in most of the "knowledge" references, this related meaning assures us that the knowledge indicated is more extensive than mere cerebral knowledge; it is a relationship of the whole person (remembering, experiencing, willing, feeling, as well as thinking) to God in all his aspects.

f. Especially, the knowledge is inconceivable without the expression in behavior which demonstrates that the God one "knows" makes an absolute claim not only on the knowing mind but on the total life of the knower. To know and not to obey is a contradiction in terms. Knowledge of the God of the Exodus that permits rebellion against his will is tantamount to idolatry.

2. The above summary partly answers the question about the relationship of the priests to the knowledge of God. As one of the essential mediators between God and his people they had to accept some responsibility for any deficiency in the relationship. In the light of the above description it can be seen that almost every facet of that relationship was the special concern of the priest. As we review the six points listed and check them against the known functions of the priest we can almost conclude that one way of defining the office of priesthood would be to speak of them as custodians of the knowledge of God. Just as the evangel is committed to the Christian evangelist, so the "knowledge" of Yahweh was entrusted to the priest. The priest, more than anyone else, was the preserver of the traditions of Israel. He was the guardian of the

Torah, in which was enshrined the knowledge of God. This fact Hosea emphasizes in 4:6d, where "the law of God" *(torah)* is paralleled with "knowledge" in v. 6b.

As keepers of the sanctuaries the priests were responsible for the cult where the traditions were enacted, where the Covenant was remembered and renewed, where the laws were received and enunciated, where the sacrifices which purified the community were performed, where the young were trained and initiated, and where prophets often preached. When priests were faithful to their calling the knowledge of God had a good chance of being secure in the land; when priests stumbled the whole land could not but stumble with them — or in Hosea's memorable phrase, "like people, like priest" (v. 9), always remembering that the onus is on the priest rather than on the people.

The plural pronouns of v. 7 originally may well have referred to the children of the priest of v. 6. It is impossible, however, to believe that they were so heard by later generations. The one priest and his sons were seen as typical of a whole generation of priests and then were seen as a cautionary tale and paradigm of the dangers necessarily inherent in the profession. The increase and development of the priesthood is good, provided the priesthood is oriented towards God. But if priests have learned to call glory, shame and shame, glory then their increase is a disaster.

Verses 7a and 8 describe a situation that most periods of history and most religions would recognize. The guardians have become unguarded, the shepherds have become wolves, but the sheep are still deceived. There exists a "cozy collaboration" between priest and people. The priests have become secularized, and instead of leading they have followed. They have found pleasure and profit in going along with the crowd and eventually in leading the crowd from the knowledge of God to the knowledge of the Baals. They provide no check on the license of the people; rather they provide them with a rationalization of their actions and a bad example. The collusion is mutually satisfying; the priests get all they want, and the people are encouraged in their sin and are not rebuked. Where there should be contention, accusation, and controversy there is peace; the ground of the conflict has been shifted. It now rests with God and his prophet (v. 4). Peace and polemic have changed places; in consequence only one result is possible. The priests will be punished and their evil deeds requited (v. 9). This punishment is not arbitrary, but is made to fit the crime in at least two ways.

The priests had forsaken the LORD for a harlotry that they believed was justified by their pseudoscience. They had discovered laws of causality and knew or thought they knew the causes of fertility, abundance, and satisfaction. To this "pure science" they had added an applied science and a technology. The system was made to work through the techniques of harlotry, that is, by "priming the pump" of agricultural production with prostitution. Part of the punishment was God's proof that their science was wrong; he would void their causal laws and demonstrate that eating actually brought hunger, and intercourse produced barren wombs (v. 10). Second, the punishment was kerygmatic, that is, a form of proclamation. Their false science arose out of their false theology. They knew gods but had no knowledge of God. So God now declares himself to be both LORD and Judge, for in the very spheres where they had denied his power he will now manifest his total control. As in ch. 2 God is shown to be in charge of all human life and determined to handle it in accordance with his moral purposes and saving plan.

4:11   To forsake God, not to know God, leads to the misuse of his gifts. Misuse of wine goes with misuse of sex. In fact the two go together. Before long the "understanding" has joined them, and they have become equally corrupt; values are in turmoil, priorities chaotic, and irrationality is the lord of misrule. Bad theology has led to bad behavior and then to madness, and then back to more bad theology, and finally to the worship of wood and reverence for a stick. Such then is the ultimate nonsense. Not to know God is not to be left godless; it is to make all things "god-able." To lose faith in God does not make one faithless; it makes one ready to believe in anything. There are no atheists in the Bible, not because its writers lived in an unsophisticated age when all men and women were "superstitious," gullible, or priest-ridden, but because they knew that all people, at all times, are in fact "religious" and that the only distinction is between those who possess the knowledge of God and those who worship idols. The message of the seraphim in Isa. 6:3 was not just "holy, holy, holy"; it was that the LORD of hosts was holy, and only he was and is holy. No doubt Hosea's contemporaries were expert in mouthing ascriptions of holiness, but like us they addressed them to the work of their own hands, to their pseudoscience, to sex, and of course to nature, the great God-substitute of their age and ours. Thus Hos. 4:13 comes very close to being a biblical version of the well-known saying "One is nearer God's heart in a garden than anywhere else on earth."

The similarities between Hosea's age and ours extend to the personification of nature, the main difference being perhaps a greater honesty in the 8th cent. B.C. In their myths that age gave names to the powers of nature, and in their rituals they overtly worshipped them. Their personification and attribution of purpose was quite open; their animism, their ascription of conscious life to inanimate objects, was shameless. One does not have to go far in some kinds of contemporary writing to discover a covert personification of that strange abstraction called "nature." Mother Nature they suggest is in control, so that "nature" determines and "nature" limits. "We must not go against nature," they say, for "nature" is the final arbiter. With such language we have all but given names and built shrines and bowed down and made offerings, even as they did in Hosea's day.

The final two phrases of v. 13 and v. 14 must be heard as addressed to the great composite audience of particular priest, priests in general, Israel, and finally of all mankind. The subject of the address is the fate of their women. The immediate historical context is the multifaceted ritual of fertility rites noted in some detail above. The form the rites took in Babylon is referred to by Herodotus as "the foulest Babylonian custom." He describes how every Babylonian woman, some time in her life, had to go to the shrine of Aphrodite and there stand in line until some stranger cast money at her and then took her aside for intercourse. Human nature being what it is, he adds "So then the women that are fair and tall are soon free to depart, but the uncomely have long to wait . . . ; for some of them remain for three years or four."

If the evidence has been interpreted correctly, the practice in Israel was not dissimilar. To woman's normal lowly status in society had been added the nameless ignominy of forced promiscuity. Women were not only chattels to be disposed of more or less at will, but they had become the raw material of a production line which turned them from human beings into things. Thus humiliated, they served the lusts of men and became the sacrificial victims of both a religion and an economy. This all-powerful combination needed their bodies in order to function efficiently, and so a religioeconomic rationale was provided to ensure that they obtained their ends. This rationale was the work of priests, and they and other males enjoyed what the women were forced to offer with a clear conscience because all was done in the name of religion. The exploitation of half the population had thus become a religious duty. Lust and oppression were offered to the LORD by seeking a blessing on foulness and so enable it to become the source of a greater blessing. Ruin is therefore destined to fall on all the people (v. 14), though not all are equally to blame. The women are wronged by the men. In a male-dominated society the plight of women is the fault of those who dominate and rule, namely, the men. Hosea's abhorrence of the state of the nation, if he had been with us today, would have forced him to add the word "pig" to the expression "male chauvinist." Moreover, it is the priests (the priesthood, the Church?) who are thus mainly responsible for the situation, because they have corrupted where they should have guarded and misled when their task was to lead.

4:15-19   In these remaining verses we are still in the realm of priestly affairs, and almost every phrase (admitting the difficulties of translation) can be understood as applying to either the ritual or to some wider aspect of the cult. Verse 15 warns against the shrines of Gilgal and Bethel, the latter being referred to by the unpleasant pun also used in Amos 5:5; for *Beth-aven* ("house of nothingness") is an insulting nickname for *Bethel* ("house of God"). The last phrase of the verse, "as the LORD lives," is a cultic oath that is now forbidden. Verse 17 is obscure. Is Ephraim to be left alone with his idolatry — allowed to stew in his own juice as it were — or is it Hosea who is to be left alone? What is not obscure is that idolatry is somehow involved. Verse 18 adds to the earlier descriptions of debauched worship, and v. 19 ends with a reference to altars or sacrifices, according to the version on which the RSV translators rely. All the verses therefore, except v. 16, make clear mention of the cult. Thus it is possible that this verse too is no exception, since the "stubborn heifer" may be a striking out at the bull images in certain sanctuaries.

In the polemic against Israel's apostasy in ch. 4 the priests and the cult have come under particular attack. Are we to conclude therefore that Hosea was opposed to both of these? Did he assume that priesthood and ritual were in themselves inimical to true religion? Was he arguing for a more "spiritual religion," devoid of burdensome impediments which contradicted the simplicities and purity of real piety? Could those today who argue for lay religion in house churches as the essential form of the Church turn to Hosea for support? I believe the answer to all these questions is patently "No." In fact the question would have been almost meaningless to anyone in the 8th cent. B.C.; it would be as fatuous as talk about incarnation without a body or about wine without a cup. The biblical faith is a mediated religion. It came into being because it was mediated from one individual to another, from the community to the individual, from one generation to another. Mediators and mediation were of its essence and the mediators par excellence were the priests, while the means of mediation were mainly to be found in the cult.

The protest, like most of the protests against kings and prophets elsewhere, was against the abuse of and not against the use or existence of the cult. It was not priesthood or liturgy or cult which drew Hosea's wrath. It was these in corrupt form when through distortion the priests were not doing what they should be doing but something else instead, often dramatically opposed to their proper objective. Hosea knew well that everything in Israel's life depended on whether there was knowledge of God in the land or not. He also knew that its presence or absence depended on whether the priest was being a true priest and the ritual was mediating what it was supposed to mediate and not something else. His attack on the offending pair, priest and ritual, was in no way aimed at their existence or raison d'être; in fact, it was exactly the opposite. His attack on them was the strongest affirmation of their importance. Humanly speaking, the faith, worship, life—indeed the very existence of the nation—depended on priest and cult being there and being what they were intended to be. The horror and bitterness displayed by Hosea indicate, not a low view of priest and altar, but the highest possible. These were a sine qua non both of Israel's present existence and of their continuity into their future relationship with Yahweh within the Covenant.

As for the Church, there is both encouragement and warning in this chapter. Heard aright, the scorn and threat both encourage and threaten. This is because our saving God has committed to the Church the things that belong to the peace of the world and the healing of the nations—not to an ideal Church or to an unburdened Church, but to the Church that comprises bishops, priests, deacons, ministers, evangelists, and teachers, the Church of sacraments and hymn books, candles and bells. These, unbelievably, are all part of the plan for the new creation. Therefore we rejoice and stand tall. But the new creation which is coming bears down upon us with an awesome judgment. The hierarchies and pulpits which can bring in the kingdom can equally hold it at bay. They can make it unlovely and undesired. They can trivialize it, denigrate it, and deny its King. They can make the plain places rough, raise great barriers, and widen the valleys. They can scatter rather than unite, confuse rather than communicate, curse rather than bless. The bread of life can become a stone and the water of life poison. Where the Church leads astray, or the Way becomes a wall, and penultimates become ultimate, then the Church has brought rejection upon itself, and darkness upon those to whom it is sent.

CHAPTER FIVE
Hosea 5:1-15

LEADERS WHO MISLEAD (5:1-7)

Whatever the origin of the parts of this poem, and however it should be divided according to the canons of literary criticism, it is generally regarded as sufficiently unified to be treated as a comprehensible unit, and a unit which continues most of the themes in ch. 4. Even some of the vocabulary is the same (compare 4:12 and 5:4). Most significant is that it is still the leadership which is under attack; but whereas ch. 4 concentrates on the priests, the accusation is now extended to include the whole establishment of authority under the monarch—priests, house of Israel, and house of the king (5:1). All in authority are responsible for Israel's loss of the knowledge of God, for the consequent loss of identity, and the coming judgment and abandonment by God. The leaders are identified with the sins of the people because they are the cause of those sins. They are also identified with the coming disaster: like leader, like people.

5:1-2　The eight lines of these verses form a satisfying pattern. They divide into two sections of four lines each, each section containing three similar statements and then a word of threat. First is the triple address to the powers that be (v. 1a, b, c) and then the unmistakable "the judgment pertains to you." The second section is rather more complicated. Three places are specified: Mizpah, Tabor, and Shittim, and in each of these places the leaders are accused in terms of the hunt. They have been a snare, a net, and a hunter's pit. The indictments are followed by the sentence of future chastisement. Presumably the three place names referred to events everyone knew about. They come to us as symbols. The far-off insignificant and forgotten event has given way to a message for all leaders and the led.

God is watching — even in Mizpah (which means "lookout point," "watchtower"), Tabor, and Shittim. And he is watching whatever the leaders do, whether religious, political, economic, or martial. And the people should watch their leaders — both with respect and suspicion, for they are bound together in the same bundle of life and rise together and fall together. If the leaders are predators, then of course the led will suffer, but in the long run so also will the marauding officials.

5:3-4   The knowledge of God, in two senses, binds these verses together and further emphasizes the links with ch. 4. The verses begin with God's knowledge of his people (an obvious assumption underlying 5:1-2), and they end with Israel's loss of the knowledge of God. Two kinds of knowledge of God are the bread of this sandwich, and what lies between? The meat of the sandwich is a description of Israel and its leaders without the knowledge of God — an Israel playing the harlot, defiled, and unable to repent and return to God. The description also includes a positive reason why Israel cannot know the God of Israel. It is because the people have changed their God for an idol—the spirit of harlotry. This new god is not only an external deity demanding obedience, but it has become internalized and taken full control. The expulsive power of a new knowledge has driven out the knowledge of God, leaving falsehood to rule.

Israel was created by covenant. Without the covenant Israel had no identity. Israel was nothing, a mere rabble of slaves. It was Jacob and not Israel—the "heel," in the popular sense of that word — before being changed by God (Gen. 32:24-32). Made by covenant Israel disintegrated without the covenant. But covenant by its very nature presumes that the partners to the union know each other. It presumes a lot more, but at the very least there must be mutual knowledge. This, says Hosea, has gone. There is now only a one-sided knowing, and that is not enough. God knows Israel—and especially he knows Israel's sins—but Israel does not know God and therefore cannot know itself. There is nothing really to know; only the sins remain. A coordinated, unified identity is no longer possible because that can only exist within the two complete knowledges of God. When God knows us and we know God, then we know who we are because then we are given a knowable identity.

5:5-7 Known but unknowing, deluded by false gods and plundering leaders, alienated Israel plunges towards inevitable destruction. Never far from the courthouse, Hosea imagines Israel defending itself in such a way that defense becomes self-accusation. Confident in their religious zeal, quite unable to see and acknowledge their apostasy, incapable of making any change of direction, the leaders address the judge with assurance of acquittal only to find that they have condemned themselves. Sentence is passed and Israel, both north and south, stumbles towards execution. The scene changes in Hos. 5:6. We are no longer in the courthouse but in the shrine where all abominations are practiced. Israel now becomes full of religious fervor, piety, and the certainty that many sacrifices will put God in a new frame of mind. How can he resist such an offering when it is made at great cost and brought with much zeal and sincerity? Weren't they seeking the LORD in the prescribed fashion? Weren't they following in Aaron's footsteps? Unfortunately they were, for Aaron had been a false leader and had brought Israel not before the face of God but to an idol. And this was what the present leadership had done; it had led Israel into the loss of God and with that to the loss of their own true identity.

How was it that they sought God and yet did not find him? Are there not at least three answers? First, they sought God in the wrong way. Sacrifices, no matter how numerous and lavish, would not guarantee access for a people who could not repent. There were ways of seeking God, but they were not this way of "flocks and herds." Second, were they really seeking the LORD, or were they seeking their own image, "the spirit of harlotry," and calling it "the LORD"? Was the real trouble not that they sought and could not find, so that their seeking had been fully rewarded? Was Israel's tragedy not this, that they always found what they were looking for, but that their search was rarely for the object for which they claimed to be looking? The third answer is the one Hosea gives. Israel could not find God because he was not available; he had withdrawn from them. It wasn't that God was not at home, that he had gone on a journey or had retired. He was at home, all right, but not to unrepentant Israel. He was there to know (v. 3) and to judge (v. 1) and to chastise (v. 2). Creation was still functioning, the sun and moon and waterfalls were still in his hands, and all were working satisfactorily. Elsewhere it was business as usual—everywhere except where Israel was concerned. To them the door was locked.

In these answers lie, almost hidden, other answers to other questions, profound questions: "Does religion not lead to God?" or "Can God be both 'at home' and 'not at home'" at once? To the first, Hosea might have answered "It all depends. How are they looking for God? Are they really looking for God or for another? Have they the will to convert, or are they imprisoned in their own past?" And can we imagine Hosea also answering with a cross-examination on what we mean by "religion." One thing that was not lacking in Hosea's time was religion. Israel's life was saturated with it. These seven verses contain several references that assume a very vigorous religious life. What was missing was not religion; rather, religion was the problem, the cause of stumbling. Something else was needed which might or might not warrant the name of "religion"; but I suspect Hosea would have refrained from any linguistic use which could conceivably have confused the knowledge of the LORD with the sort of practices Israel had in common with the Canaanites —or with anyone else for that matter.

The second question is one already dealt with above. God is present in his world in two ways. He is known in creation and in redemption; in nature he is known "naturally," in salvation by faith. Hosea expresses this truth in yet another form: the ubiquitous God has withdrawn from Israel.

Why has God withdrawn? It was not caprice or spite, or loss of love or interest. It was the inevitable act of God. It was the withdrawal demanded by love. The love that had chosen freely and given freedom to the chosen one could never do less than honor that freedom. Israel the partner in covenant had broken the covenant; Israel the wife had been unfaithful (v. 7a, b); Israel the known was unknowing. It was Israel who had first withdrawn from God, and God's withdrawing was the inevitable response. God's absence was a deprivation and a punishment; it was both educational and designed to bring a change in Israel's attitude. Yet these are still not the profoundest reasons for God's locked door. They do not justify the word "inevitable"; rather, they are secondary to something far more fundamental. The true cause of God's absence was that love cannot coerce, and God loved Israel. Creators can coerce, partners can enforce, kings can command and educationalists overrule, but lovers knock on locked doors and then go away (Cant. 5:2ff.). It is the seducer or rapist who stays. A withdrawn Israel, in the nature of things, learns of a withdrawn

God, but God's withdrawing is not primarily vengeful nor a simple tit for tat. It is the work of suffering love.

But injured love injures in return, not because it has turned to hate but because it is love that still hopes. One expression of its hope is the belief that injury can still be felt, that the faithless one is not dead to all pain but can still be moved, and that the movement will one day be towards the one deserted. This explains the final line of Hos. 5:7: "Now the new moon shall devour them with their fields." The withdrawn God punishes, but the punishment flows from love and is designed to reawaken love.

The promised punishment baffles us if we try to understand it in precise logical terms. New moons do not eat fields. But a new moon can stand for cultic celebration, for religious feast and festival, and the reference is most appropriate if the celebration has more than a touch of sexual significance. And fields can stand for the fruits of fertility, the result of blessing and of all the things that the cult was designed to ensure. The cult was the means of production, and the fields represented the produce and the workers' reward. So God's loving punishment (as so often in Hosea) was to turn the system upside down. Israel finds yet another example of God's irony as once more the cause does not produce the expected result. "New moons" are meant to produce fields ripe unto harvest and food for the people to devour. Instead they do the opposite. The system has backfired; it is the fields that are devoured, and the "new moons" have done the devouring.

GOD AND A CIVIL WAR (5:8-15)

Hosea 5:8 with its call to arms is the beginning of a new section, and in it we are faced unavoidably with two questions. The first concerns the historical context of the following verses; the second asks about the relationship existing between the separate parts.

1. In 1919 Albrecht Alt wrote an article which proposed that Hos. 5:8–6:6 could best be understood against the background of the Syro-Ephraimite War which is reported in 2 Kgs. 16 and Isa. 7 ("Hosea 5:8-6:6, ein Krieg und seine Folgen in prophetischer Beleuchtung," repr. in *Kleine Schriften,* 2 [Munich: C. H. Beck, 1959], 163-187). His arguments have been extremely influential and with some modifications have determined the views of a majority of commentators. Only a minority rejects the proposal en-

tirely, yet some others not only accept it but extend it and would include all of Hos. 5:8–8:1 as coming from the same historical context and possessing the same themes.

2. Related to the first question is the one of unity. Here the opinions are legion. Reference to most of the varied views is unnecessary in this commentary, but not all can be avoided because sometimes the interconnectedness or otherwise of the parts can make a crucial difference to our interpretation. Only in such instances need we examine the connecting links; otherwise we shall pursue the "canonical" policy already adopted and assume that we have not been left with a collection of disparate fragments.

5:8-15   In 5:8 Hosea is Israel's watchman. An attack is being made on the north by Judah, and Hosea sounds the alarm as the invading forces move relentlessly northward. They advance from Jerusalem to Gibeah, then continue the 3 km. (2 mi.) on to Ramah, and finally arrive at Bethel. The invaders pass through Benjamin territory, which presumably belonged to Israel during the 8th century.

Perhaps Hosea was standing on the city walls. Despatches are at hand, and perhaps he can even see the approaching Judean forces. Whatever the actual circumstances, he was on the alert—acting as society's sentry. The prophet is called to be awake, vigilant, and to see the danger before it is too late to prepare resistance. So Hosea warns, but he also prepares. He is recruiting sergeant as well as sentry, for the horn, trumpet, and alarm will muster the troops. Here was a prophet who did more than talk.

Verse 8 begins a new section but also links with v. 7, which had ended with a threat. Now the threat is almost upon them. In v. 9 the prophet-sentry becomes the mouth of the LORD as the true explanation of what is happening is given. Hosea's hearers learn that this is no ordinary war; the enemy is not merely brother-Judah. The real enemy is God himself, for it is he who is bringing the desolation upon that section of his people known as Ephraim. Hosea is extremely careful about names. As a prophet he speaks to the tribes of Israel (i.e., to all twelve tribes), even though he lives among the northern ones. In the present situation, as the spokesman to all the tribes, he has to announce that God is using part of Israel (Judah) to punish another part (Ephraim). The chosen are divided, but in this division it is not a simple case of one being right and the other wrong. God is acting (quite differently) on both sides, and neither side has much to be proud of. Ephraim is being made desolate for their sins, and the fact that Judah is the instrument of desolation does not exempt them from blame and automatically put them on the side of God. The leaders of Judah are very culpable; they are in fact accused by God for being "like those who remove the landmark" (Deut. 27:17), and equally with Ephraim they will be made to suffer. God will pour out his wrath like water upon them. The explanation of Ephraim's oppression continues in Hos. 5:11. The oppression has already begun because of Israel's determination "to go after vanity." The word "vanity" (or "worthlessness" or "nothingness" or even "excreta") translates a word found also in the drunkard's jingle in Isa. 28:10, 13. The precise reference is not clear. Is it a reference to Ephraim's trust in Damascus or in Egypt? In other words, it is a political nonsense. Or is it a religious "vanity" because it indicates Ephraim's trust in the gods of Canaan? The exact referent is unknown and the questions are not very important as the "vanity" must be defined in terms of alternatives to God. Whether Ephraim is trusting in other nations more than in God or whether they have replaced him with myths is not of major significance. Whatever is meant by "vanity," the statement is about the opposite to vanity: about God the true reality, the true absolute, the wholly trustworthy.

There now follows one of Hosea's "therefores." As we found in Hos. 2, these cannot be taken lightly. This "therefore" introduces one of the harshest statements to be found in any prophetic book. God is the "moth" (or the 'pus') in Ephraim. He is like dry rot to the house of Judah. The prophet who speaks most of the love of God is the one who speaks of God's judgment in the most unlovely language. He is saying in effect "Don't look for any other cause of your country's disasters; don't waste time diagnosing. I can already tell you what the post mortem will produce. Here is the coroner's report. The victim died of an unusual ailment: God!" The germ, with the resulting wasting and corruption, was—God!!

This understanding of the nature of the sickness provides almost all the explanation required to exegete 5:13 and 14. Ephraim and Judah have eyes to see the sickness and the wound because they are writ large in the horrors of war, but their powers of diagnosis are more than feeble; they wholly mislead. On the assumption that they are faced with the normal bacillae of politics and war they secure the normal remedies. They appeal to Assyria. For relief from rape and slaughter they turn to one of history's most brutal oppressors. This is an insane enough thing to do, but a greater madness is still to be revealed. As though it were not bad enough to go to the butcher when one needs a doctor, the ultimate madness was in thinking that anyone could conquer an illness which had been brought on by God. Political and martial medicine is for political and military patients. Victims of the God-cancer need a very different type of cure.

The pronoun is emphasized as God declares in v. 14 "For *I* will be like a lion . . . a young lion. . . ." Just in case his listeners had not been able to believe what they had heard in v. 12, the same points are restated in no less horrendous language. The loving, redeeming God is now likened to lions at their fiercest—when they are young and hungry. It is God and none other who kills and rends, apparently without compunction or compassion, because after the slaughter he leaves the bloody scene, presumably to digest at leisure. The lion simile is appropriate to describe how Assyria walked the imperial path, but it is surely an astounding way to speak of the God who in ch. 11 speaks of Israel as his son. Ours not to reason why, or to explain. It is the Scriptures (in their entirety) which witness to our justification. We cannot and should not attempt to justify the source of all that enables us to be justified. We shall be content to remark on a paradox so often found in both Old and New Testaments, namely, that it is often those who most stress one pole of God's activity who are most likely to be aware of and underline the other pole. It is done with no sense of contradiction, and even the tension is rarely discussed. The gentle Jesus, meek and mild, who nevertheless can speak of the agonies of hell as no other does, is prefigured in the words of many of his forerunners. It is almost as though the goodness of God cannot be seen without his severity, as though he cannot be known as savior unless he has been feared as enemy. Hosea is one of many who prepared us for the day when God's own Son cried "My God, my God, why hast thou forsaken me" before he was able confidently to commit his soul into his Father's hands.

The final verse (5:15) is a comment on the awful news preceding it and a preparation for what is to follow in ch. 6. God's "going away" and "carrying off" are shown not to be the whole story. They are scenes in a drama which need the later acts for clarification. The "going away" is real, but it is only disciplinary; it is chastisement with a saving purpose. In the same way, just as God goes away only because the people had gone from him, so his return is dependent on their turning once more to him. The brutality received at the hands of Judah or Assyria is a "godly" brutality; it is designed to bring confession of guilt, a change of heart, and a renewal of the covenant as the lost sheep return to the fold.

One commentator, in referring to the section beginning at 5:8, uses the phrase "war among brothers" to describe the conflict between Ephraim and Judah (James Luther Mays, *Hosea,* 85ff.). The warring halves of Israel did not limit their warfare to the events in question. Theirs was a history of hostility and animosity with deep roots and which continued, perhaps even into the Judea/Samaria bitterness of NT times. I refer to this for two reasons.

1. This example of fratricidal strife is one example of a theme found in other places in Scripture beginning with Cain and Abel and persisting through Isaac and Ishmael, Jacob and Esau, Joseph and his brothers. "War among brothers" is a common subject in Scripture. Is this noteworthy in any way, or merely of antiquarian interest? Since Karl Marx's writings began to influence all the world's thinking it has been increasingly fashionable to assume that many of society's ills were caused by class warfare, that in fact class struggle has been the fundamental problem of our life together. Does the biblical concern with warring brothers question this assumption? Would the two Testaments support the Marxist diagnosis, or would they point rather to fraternal hatred—the battle between peers, between like and like—rather than class conflict, as our fundamental disease?

2. If this is so, then there is something for our comfort in Hosea's writings because he shows us that God is at work even in fratricidal strife. The bitter civil war Hosea is writing about is not totally distanced from the God who is working his purposes out. Rather, God is there in the midst of it, right in the vicious heart of it. He is there judging, punishing, rending, destroying—not aloof or abstracted from it, but caught up and involved in an educative plan which springs from love and moves to repentance, renewal, and redemption. God is not at the mercy of sibling rivalry; on the contrary, murdering brothers have a place in God's mercy. Can the same be said for the class war diagnosis? Does the prophetic analysis give us hope where it is most needed, when other theories mislead?

CHAPTER SIX
Hosea 6:1-11a

TURN AGAIN, ISRAEL (6:1-6)

The previous chapter ended with God's refusal to return unless Israel took the first moves towards reconciliation. Hosea 6:1 begins with a call from within Israel demanding that they should return. So is this the end of the story? Is the mission of the prophet accomplished? Is all well? Did Israel really repent and with contrite hearts return? These and many other questions turn on our understanding of vv. 1-3. Where do these verses come from? What do they mean? And how do they connect with vv. 4-6? And why does RSV add the word "saying"?

On the surface vv. 1-3 express everything that could be wished for. Israel had decided to come home. The prodigal has learned his lesson. God's way of chastening those whom he loves has worked; the punishment has produced the desired effect. The God who tears can heal, the batterer can equally well bandage (v. 1), and the complete cure is almost at hand. Two or three days at the most and then they will be enjoying life more abundantly (v. 2). The great confidence in God's faithfulness continues into v. 3 and is partly matched by Israel's urgency to "know the LORD." Note how in Isaiah and Psalms this picture of spring rains is also used. If only the book of Hosea ended here all would be well, but it doesn't. The tale of sin is a long one, and even more crushing than the succeeding account of disobedience is the content of the next three verses (Hos. 6:4-6). These are a divine word of accusation against Israel, condemning Israel's love and likening it to morning mist and early dew. In other words it was not an enduring love; it was not *hesed*, the RSV's "steadfast love," but ephemeral and could in the nature of things only draw upon itself the treatment detailed in v. 5. Finally v. 6 describes what God really requires from those in covenant with him. If vv. 4-6 are quite independent of the preceding verses, then vv. 1-3 can be read as a sincere desire to return. If, on the other hand, the six verses are a unit then we must assume gross deficiency in the first three of them.

I propose to take the six verses as continuous and, therefore, to accept that the first three express a superficial repentance. This proposal has nothing to do with the time of origin or the original intention expressed in any of the parts. On these questions we have to keep an open mind. Verses 1-3 may possibly be satire; they may be from a contemporary liturgy, used in public worship; they may be Hosea's own construction or be the work of a priest or of an unknown third party. We just do not know. What we must note is proximity of the passage to the traditional text in vv. 4-6 and the total absence of any historical reference which might incline us to divide the verses into two distinct halves. In fact the evidence is rather against such a division, as there seems to be a correspondence in verse form yet in contrast to their contents. Verses 1 and 4 correspond in that both speak of God's intention and of Israel's motivation yet in very different terms. Verses 2 and 5 are similar in that they both speak of God's acts, but from opposing points of view. Verses 3 and 6 describe Israel's response and what God is like, but in wholly dissimilar language. We conclude, therefore, that the six verses describe Israel's "return" as a sham, or at least as an inadequate confession; that is why the return is followed by God's exposure of its hollow triviality and then his giving of his own definition of what is demanded of his people.

6:1-3   We read these verses then as having the form of godliness but little, if any, of the necessary substance. All the right words are used: Israel will return to the LORD as they are invited to do, because they are confident that God is their healer and the great physician (v. 1). The language used is unexceptional. Similarly with v. 2: the healing God surely longs to heal, and the living God gives life so that humans can live before him. Who can complain at such sentiments, or protest when in v. 3 the penitents affirm that God's nature is as certain as the laws of nature (dawn, showers, rain)? And safe in this assurance, who dare object that they should "press on to know the LORD"? Only a very suspicious mind would imagine that all this was mere window dressing and that it is only God's response in what follows (does God have a very suspicious mind?) that forces us today to read these lines again. When we do so, we begin to detect a new note.

Does v. 1 now show us a nation in distress, prepared to do anything to find relief? They now know where the real trouble lies—with God! He has made this quite clear in ch. 5, so why should they not try to meet him on his own terms? But the terms are beyond them. They may think they understand them and can conform to them; but what they in fact produce is not evidence of trust and contrition, but a demonstration merely of belief in "cheap grace." What they are saying is something like "Let's go home; God will put things right. That's what he is there for—to hear and to forgive. That's his job, isn't it?"

The next verse (v. 2) now sounds overconfident and reveals a very presumptuous trust in a kindly old grandfather rather than in a father—and what is more, a grandfather who is dependent on his grandchildren! They are "to live before him" and to see to his needs. The final verse (v. 3) with its nature references perhaps should be seen not so much as a witness to confident belief in the God who had revealed himself in history. Rather, it should be seen as a confession that their effective faith is not in Israel's God at all but in the nature gods of Canaan who are identified with the dawn and the showers and the rain. Some such understanding is demanded by and prepares us for the next three verses.

6:4-6   We see immediately that the view of God merely as disease or as a ravening lion is only partial (5:12); it is more a description of function than of essence. In 6:4, however, we come close to discovering his essential nature. The first two lines foreshadow the amazing passage in 11:8 where the goodness and the severity of God are maintained in conflict; but already in the present verse we are permitted a glimpse into the mind of God and a glimpse of the dialogue within the "heart" of God that Hosea is permitted to eavesdrop.

The prophet is someone who has stood in the council of God and heard the final decree. He is sometimes permitted to sit in the "visitors' gallery," so to speak, and to hear the debate proceeding (Isa. 6; Job 1-2; 1 Kgs. 22), during which the heavenly beings are called upon to contribute suggestions, reports, and advice. Hosea takes us a step further as he reports on the deliberations that actually go on in the mind of the Godhead. The two questions with which the present section begins—about how God should deal, first with Ephraim, and then with Judah—reveal to us much about God, about how he treats his chosen ones, and also about how these chosen ones respond in certain circumstances.

1. God's actions in human history are shown not to be automatic reactions, predetermined mechanistic movements when faced by unusual (or usual) events. God's response is personal; the pros and cons are weighed in the balance. There appears to be what in humankind might be taken for indecision and uncertainty, perhaps even doubt. I assume that what we are being introduced to is a decision-making process which delays the final judgment until all the evidence is in. "The more haste, the less justice" might be one of the principles involved. Another is "When in doubt give priority to compassion." Is it a temptation or an insight to see in these brief dialogues a little pushing at the boundaries of OT monotheism, a hesitant preparation for the NT teaching about the trinity? Whatever else is in them, there is a clear word for the Church's mission. We do not proclaim a computer-God or a fiscal system. Nor do we announce a principle or an indirect impersonal force. There is no pressing of numbers nor is there the immediate appearance of a predetermined conclusion as if on a screen. Rather we meet with a father passionately but carefully seeking the best for the children he calls by name.

2. Ephraim and Judah were constantly at each other's throats, yet God somehow was present with both of them, judging as well as redeeming each of them. Both stand there before God; both will receive what is right for them, but what they get may be very different. Equal concern is shown for the pair of them. They receive an assurance of absolute justice but with no certainty of identical treatment. As we know, their two histories after the time of Hosea were vastly different. Ephraim ceased to exist in any recognizable form. Despite having to live through tremendous vicissitudes Judah (or Judea, as it came to be known) continued at least long enough to receive him whom the Church has hailed to be the Messiah. A great discrepancy, an intolerable unfairness this, we might protest, to which the biblical retort may well be that this is the true fairness—the true egalitarianism in its perfect and absolute form.

3. Christians today frequently speak of "dialogue." Does the Bible do so? If so, does the Bible provide us with signposts and directions to guide us as we continue with the dialogue? If we are

prepared to give a broad connotation to the word "dialogue," we can confidently reply that the Bible contains many types of dialogue. Scripture records dialogue between God and mankind, between God and the people of God. It includes dialogues between prophet and king, prophet and priest, prophet and people. And much of revelation comes to us as beads strung on a thread, a picture which might portray the dialogue between the people of God and the nations. But what weight do we give to all such dialogue? More is given to some occurrences than to others, inevitably; yet we must grant a very significant place to it because we find dialogue to be deep in the being of God himself. The center of all things is not silent stillness but a conversation. Hosea obviously had been made aware that in the beginning was the Word.

The reason for God's inner struggle is provided in the second half of the verse, which likens Israel's love to "a morning cloud" and to "dew that goes early away." We must pause on the word "love" *(hesed)*. It is significant that it is deficient love that God concentrates on here. It is the cause of the violence seen in v. 5 and it reoccurs as what God "requires" in v. 6. Why? Israel's fine sounding confession in vv. 1-3 makes no promise of such love; they were then seeking to *know* the LORD and not to *love* him. Two points are to be made at this stage.

1. Love and knowledge are distinguishable but almost inseparable. They are both responses to God, who has revealed himself to Israel through the events of their history and especially through the Exodus events. Love and knowledge are both related to the Covenant and can hardly be conceived apart from it, and they both find expression in obedient behavior and faithfulness. Therefore, the scathing comments on Israel's love certainly imply that the knowledge they were looking for was deficient, equally of their own imagining, and not what God required.

2. The central concern of all scripture is mankind's relationship with God. The Bible is full of "topics," but there is really only one "subject" in it. The NT expresses it as "God was in Christ reconciling the world to himself"—the world being the world of mankind. The central issue in the OT also is the re-creative, reconciling love of the faithful God. Love grows from the healed relationship. Love is what is made possible by forgiveness, what cements the Covenant from which flow both thankfulness and obedience. Love of God engenders love of neighbor, breaks down barriers,

repudiates idolatry, casts out fear. Love is central to all else. In emphasizing love Hosea has not neglected other virtues; he has merely enabled them to find their rightful place.

The love of which God speaks is a love required by the Covenant. It is the Hebrew word *hesed,* as in 2:19, and not *ahabah,* as in Deut. 6:5. It is the kind of love one has for the other member in a partnership because he or she has promised to love. It is a commitment of the will and not a function of the emotions, and it is intended to last as long as the partnership lasts. Indeed the partnership cannot last without it. Instead of this kind of love Israel offers a counterfeit love, one which, based on the worship of the gods of ever-changing nature, is as short-lived as the mists and dews of nature. That kind of love is unrelated to any covenant; it is of the emotions and not of the will, and it is short-lived. Such love is a mere whim, a fancy, "cotton wool not cornerstone." Predictably such a description of it is followed by another "therefore" and a reminder by God of what such pseudolove has provoked in the past.

The comments on Hos. 6:4 above have introduced the subject of God's word and of its power. The theme continues in v. 5, where it is greatly reinforced. God's words of woe and welfare were entrusted particularly to the prophets. It is almost a definition of a prophet to describe him as someone charged to declare the word of God. Moreover, this charge made the prophet almost Godlike in the eyes of the people, because the word he spoke was not merely a word of report or of information but was a word that brought into being the events it announced. Words of joy created happenings of delight, whereas words of judgment brought execution of the sentence pronounced; and words of warfare mustered the enemies' forces, razed cities, and shed blood. Such a view of God's active, creative, self-fulfilling word lies behind the statements of v. 5. God hews and slays by the word committed to the prophet. This is more than metaphor and cannot be compared with anything found in modern Western usage. Readers from more traditional cultures are better able to understand what Hosea means (for example, I found this to be so in Taiwan). Words of curse and blessing, with their power actually to bring about what the speaker has enunciated in language, are rarely idle pronouncements in many communities. They are to be taken seriously. Being powerful, they are not to be taken lightly even if sometimes they are spoken lightly

—or even mistakenly. A word mispronounced so that it sounds like "death" can become a hazard. Once uttered it can become independent of the intention or control of the speaker. It then possesses a life of its own, like a wayward missile.

The word of God committed to the prophet however is not wayward. It is held on a tight rein and wholly controlled by the intention of God. It does not deviate unless he wishes it to; and if he so wishes, a curse can become a blessing or a blessing turn into a curse. Or the whole utterance can be withdrawn. In v. 5 Hosea may have had in mind specific prophets such as Elijah, Elisha, or Micaiah ben Imlah, or even Amos. Whoever they were, their message was one of condemnation and woe that could provide models for Hosea's announcement of "hewing" and "slaying" in v. 5a, b. Does the same mood then continue on into the final phrase "my ('thy' in Hebrew) judgment goes forth as the light"? Is it denunciatory judgment that is referred to here? Or is there a hint of something else beyond the affliction, as is so often the case in Hosea? The answers come in two parts.

1. Whatever is intended here, it is in contrast with Israel's love which cannot stand the light of day. Morning mist and morning dew both fly before the sun's light, and God's judgment is like the going forth of the sun. Whether the contrast is merely with regard to matters of power and constancy or whether the "judgment" is opposed in every way to frail Israel's deceptive love is hard to say, but perhaps the meaning is already hinted at in the comparison.

2. The word for "judgment," *mishpat,* refers to the right order in society. Right order and right relationships naturally assume that evil gets its deserts and wrongdoers are punished, so the judgment referred to is certainly condemnatory. But is it only condemnatory? *Mishpat* is also a component of peace *(shalom)* and right order, and right relationships include much of what constitutes a healthy society. We conclude, therefore, that this final phrase looks beyond the "hewing" and "slaying" and forward to something more hopeful.

Verse 6 is the climax of this section. It also provides an explanation of much that precedes it and forms a basis for the major part of what follows. What God desires is love, not sacrifice, and knowledge of himself, not burnt offerings. What does this mean positively?

1. Worship must be focused on the God who has revealed him-

self in Israel's history. The love and the knowledge spoken of are
not love and knowledge in general. They cannot be separated from
the Exodus and the Covenant which is associated with it. These
words, *hesed* and *da'at,* speak of a specific kind of love and of
knowledge with a special and specific object (Yahweh), known
only in the special and specific ways in which he has appeared to
Israel.

2. God has not only appeared in history and in specific ways.
He has spoken about his appearing in specific words given to
specific people. Obedience to these words is an essential element
in the Covenant. There is no substitute for them.

3. The response to the actions and the words of God must be a
personal response, a self-giving, a self-commitment. Nothing else
will do. There are no substitutes for "all your heart, and soul, and
strength, and mind."

What does the verse mean negatively?

1. Worship must not be of the gods that humans make for themselves in the likeness of the works of nature. It must not be directed
to the general, to the universal, to all creation, or even to any part
of all creation. Worship is not for the purpose of satisfying a
hungry, thirsty, lusty natural god or goddess. Worship is not to be
understood as feeding living creatures into the jaws of necessity,
caprice, and brutality.

2. The God who has spoken clearly, giving his people unambiguous directions, is the God who repudiates all religion that is a
mere response to something else. *"Hesed"* and *"mishpat,"* based as
they are on the word of God and as demanded by the word of God,
are the denial and rejection of all voices that would claim to speak
with absolute authority. Faiths that rest on personal opinion or personal inclination, on myth, on passion, on culture, on philosophy
or fear or fiction, on nation or nature are outlawed.

3. God's desire for love and knowledge permits no response that
is impersonal. Entrance into God's community cannot be bought;
the door cannot be forced. Riches, power, birth, breeding, face,
fame, fortune, or fate have no visa that God's kingdom recognizes.
There are no substitutes for the strong devotion of loyal and steadfast love and of knowledge of God.

Does Hosea allow no place for sacrifice in Israel's worship? This
is the same question that must be addressed to Samuel (1 Sam.
15:22), Amos (Am. 5:21), Isaiah (Isa. 1:12-17), Micah (Mic. 6:6-

8), and others. Not one of those questioned provides an unambiguous answer because they were never confronted with this question. If we insist on posing precisely this question we must be satisfied with an answer that is only a guess. My guess is that Hosea was not rejecting all sacrifice per se; rather, he was condemning its abuse. Most Protestants who have opposed the Roman Catholic Mass would have been horrified if they had been misunderstood as rejecting the sacraments or denying the importance of the Lord's Supper. Their opposition was to a presumed misuse that was not a true one. I think Hosea's viewpoint was similar. Sacrifices which hindered love and knowledge or had become substitutes for them had to be resisted and rooted out because they were not benefiting what they were supposed to benefit. On the other hand, sacrifices offered within the context of the whole law of the Covenant which existed by and for the love and knowledge of God would have had his full support.

THE JOURNEY NOT MADE (6:7-11a)

The seminal explanatory statement has been made in Hos. 6:6. Between vv. 6 and 7 there is a change of step, but on the whole the same themes continue and are possibly present with little alteration until the end of ch. 7. God's unchanging purpose, constantly thwarted by Israel's rebellion and refusal to keep covenant, dominates the poems. Leaders and people are jointly culpable, and both their devotions and their diplomacy are expressions of internal idolatry. Where individual poems or strophes within poems begin and end is uncertain, and any divisions we make are unavoidably arbitrary. In some verses the uncertainty extends to the meaning of the text, and informed guesses are in some cases almost as much guess as information.

6:7-9 Verses 7-9 are linked together by the mention of three place names (Adam [a city in the Jordan valley], Gilead, and Shechem), by villainy throughout, and possibly also by continued invective against the priests. The priests are clearly attacked in v. 9, and the "they" in v. 7 might refer to them also. The priest might also still be present in v. 10 if the "house of Israel" really means the shrine at Bethel, as it well might. These three verses, with their opening remarks about covenant, follow naturally after the statement of v. 6, for everything in them implies "Covenant." The "Covenant" (or "marriage," because the two are interchangeable in Hosea; see chs. 1 and 2) was something contracted outside Canaan. It had been promised in Egypt and ratified in the wilderness at Sinai (Exod. 24). Part of its provision (with roots going back to Abraham) was the land of promise, Canaan. But what had happened when the tribes came to dwell in Canaan? How did Israel receive the gracious Covenant gift? Hosea tells us now. They turned it into a land of rebellion and turned against the gracious Giver. Everywhere—Adam, Gilead, Shechem, etc., etc.—the story was the same: transgression, faithlessness, evil, bloodshed, robbery, murder, villainy. And who were largely to blame? The priests who themselves were another gracious gift and who were supposed to be the preservers of the Covenant. God gives; Israel either throws his gift away or turns it into a weapon to be used against God, just as they had done with the gift of sacrifice!

Hosea's hearers would have understood the geographical references. Almost certainly the prophet is reminding them of contemporary events which were of sufficient magnitude or near enough in time to make further elaboration unnecessary. To mention the place is enough. But every place has a history, and every name has an aura. These cities were no exception. Shechem had been an early cultic center (Josh. 8:30-31); Gilead had known bloodshed before (1 Kgs. 2:5); and could the double meaning of Adam be lost on anyone? Surely transgression at a place named Adam was given greater significance as people thought of another Adam and of that first transgression recounted in Gen. 3. Since the contemporary context can only be a matter of speculation, does this mean that we are unable to interpret the verses as they should be interpreted? If the contemporary historical context were essential to our understanding, presumably the editors would have provided it rather than merely transmitting matters that would remain eternally opaque. Their view of biblical interpretation must have been consistent with an absence of historical background. Maybe the final editors did not know the context of his references to these three places, and almost certainly it was unknown to the Jewish "canonizers" of the OT, even as it was unknown later to the Christian "canonizers" of the whole Bible. We must read these place names, therefore, without too much regard to their history and even their geography. They are representative of the whole land and of the whole people of Israel. They have become symbols that speak of universal disobedience. In these places and everywhere else, says the prophet, Israel's response to God's desire for love and knowledge (Hos. 6:6) has been to do exactly the opposite. It was left to a later Christian writer to coin the phrase "total depravity"; these and other verses demonstrate that its content was known only too well to Hosea.

6:10-11a I shall assume that this particular section is now rounded off by Hos. 6:10 and 11a (but see the Jerusalem Bible for another view) and shall not inquire too concernedly about the date and authorship of v. 11a. If it is a later addition, as I suspect, it may have greater meaning for us than if it were original to Hosea. However, there are several questions to be asked. The first arises from the fact that these verses include three place names. Does this mean that they are a continuation of the list in vv. 7-9, or do they serve a different function? Verse 10 with its additions to the account of Israel's sins might support the former suggestion (i.e., just "more of the same"). Verse 11a with its threatened "harvest" suggests that something else is intended. I take both of the verses as having a concluding function. "House of Israel," "Ephraim," and "Judah" do not fit easily into the series "Adam," "Gilead," and "Shechem." They represent the general rather than the particular, the whole and not the part. Verse 10 reads more like a summary and as such confirms the interpretation given above that the three localities stand for the totality of God's erring people. Thus in two ways vv. 7-10 give the judgment that all Israel has responded in like manner to God's desire. In the first of these (vv. 7-9) specific examples are given of shocking behavior that is nevertheless representative of the whole country. The second is to speak of the whole country directly ("house of Israel," "Ephraim") and to predicate of their faith and life the great general comprehensive term which Hosea has made his own: harlotry.

The sentence about Judah (v. 11a) provides a different kind of ending. First, it is a warning against complacency. If Judah has sown the same seed as Ephraim (and they had) then they could expect the same harvest, sooner or later, as their northern counterpart. Disaster falling on Ephraim must be seen not as something to rejoice in, but as the shadow of a further disaster—the one that will come on Judah. Second, v. 11a forms a conclusion meant for all succeeding readers and not only for contemporary Judah. Obviously in the first place it was uttered as a warning to Judah; perhaps it was written by a Judean scribe anxious to draw the moral clearly even though a touch pedantically and didactically. But whoever the author, he has made it quite clear that the words of Hosea possess unchanged value and were not uttered only for their own day. In later ages in differing contexts, although with very differing harmonies, they would sound the same tune. Thus the word to ancient Judah is still emphatically a word about our complacency and our apostasy, even about our harvest if we do not return.

Throughout ch. 6 runs the theme of repentance—its necessity and the total inability of Israel to produce it. Chapter 5 ends with a call for repentance. Chapter 6 begins with the form but not the substance of it; Israel is then condemned, and the rest of the chapter outlines either what happens to the impenitent people or what emerges out of their state of impenitence. Looking now at v. 11b and its continuation into ch. 7, we note that this subject is still with us. God is constantly turning to Israel; but Israel, though sometimes turning to God and occasionally even sparing him a thought, cannot really return. The effort is beyond their powers, even if they had the will to do so—which they do not possess.

Why then does God not desist and give up this hopeless struggle? In the face of such monumental self-satisfaction and moral weakness, why does he actually persevere as he does? Why does he not "cut his losses" and "begin again"? The answer comes finally in ch. 11. He perseveres because he is God and not human; but even before the answer is given in that form, it is already present in other guises. It is because God has "married" Israel; God has made a covenant with her, God has bound himself in righteousness, justice, steadfast love, mercy, and faithfulness to Israel (Hos. 2:19-20). Having gone so far he has found himself in a dilemma. God's "wife" must be worthy of her "husband." That is why there sounds the absolute demand for a total turning to God and for incontrovertible evidence of the fruits of repentance. At the same time there is here an awareness of how feeble and wayward Israel is with no hope of any turning that is more than a dream. This realization accounts for God's infinite patience and final succour. God's dilemma produces a paradoxical treatment of his people: forever casting off but never letting go, always punishing to save, killing to make alive. He is "easy to please but hard to satisfy" as George MacDonald has said.

From the human side we see not so much a paradox as sheer frailty and lack of integration and integrity. For God and for his prophets, to know was to do. How could anyone know the true God and worship idols? How could anyone know justice and do unjustly? Such questions lie behind all the prophetic writings. Similarly, God and his servants are puzzled that humans do not grasp what they reach for, do not do what they will, and do not will what they desire. Hosea found a people that had not consciously willed to depart from God; they had just drifted and were at sea. They thought sometimes of the harbor and they possessed all the necessary maps, but the journey was never made; or, if started, before long there was a change of direction. The harbor was never reached. Israel was often homesick but found it impossible to make the journey. But still the paradoxical Father in all his loving contrition waits and waits. Patience demanded in fact a wait of several hundred years before a great new hope arose and before a prodigal son not only felt homesick but found the will and the power to make the journey home.

POETIC JUSTICE
Hosea 6:11b–7:16

This chapter concludes Section II of the prophecy, which we take to be an account of Israel's current condition resulting from their lack of the knowledge of God and their inability to take the steps necessary to rectify the situation. The chapter is plainly continuous with chs. 4–6, but new features appear as the argument develops.

The RSV translation attaches 6:11b to ch. 7. This is acceptable and makes good sense. It also helps to complete a discernible structure within the chapter which, although perhaps not originally intended, does not do violence to the content; rather it provides a form which enables the context to be more easily grasped. The whole divides into four parts: 6:11b-7:2; 7:3-7; 7:8-12; 7:13-16. Of these, the first and the fourth are similar, as are the second and third. The first and the last are laments from the mouth of God, so that the style and form are comparable. Also, they are concerned with the covenantal aspect of Israel's circumstances, that is, with the relationships between God and Israel on which all else depends. Parts two and three deal with political matters. The former concentrates on internal affairs and in particular on the intrigue and violence that surround the tottering monarchy. The latter turns to external problems, especially the diplomatic maneuvering that the threat of war had prompted. We have then, sandwiched between covenantal concerns, two layers of the political; or between the "religious," the ethical; between the vertical, the horizontal; between the God/human relationship, the human/human relationship. The form of the poem is accordingly expressive of its content. The outward in some measure reveals the inward, because the message of the passage is that human existence is a unity in which the things of earth cannot be divorced from our dealings with heaven. (Here the Prophets are in total disagreement with the philosophers of Greece, but they would be fully understood by the peoples of the Pacific). There are no autonomous regions, no walled gardens that are not part of the estate, and the lord of the estate is God. To him we owe obedience before all else, and on our standing with him depends everything we do—even king-making and international treaties.

6:11b–7:2   The last words to Israel and Judah in ch. 6 had been about their harlotry and defilement. These followed other accusations which included bloodshed, murder, and villainy. The present poem begins with a lament from God that bemoans Israel's frustration of all God's plans to redeem them. God's dilemma at not being able to do as he wishes is not unlike the brief dialogue with himself in 6:4; and what he wants to do—namely, restore Israel's fortunes and heal them—is his response to the "confession" in 6:1-3. The expression translated "restore the fortunes" consists of the double use of a verb that means "turn"; a literal translation would be something like "turn the turning" or "return the returning," which is not very helpful. Perhaps it is of help to point out that the verb is the one used by some OT writers when they call upon Israel to return to God, that is, to repent. Did Hosea deliberately choose this verb, not only to introduce the theme of penitence, but also to hint that in repenting Israel would not be dependent merely on their own resources? It would be God who would be doing the "turning the turning" in order to restore Israel's fortunes. Such an interpretation is supported by the use in the parallel line of the verb "to heal." This verb in Hosea includes the ideas of forgiveness and redemption.

Here God demonstrates that he is easy to please (though hard to satisfy) by his indulgent response to what he knows is a deceptive confession and appeal in 6:1-3. He is all ready to forgive and heal; but his loving gesture turns to lament, even as the gesture is made. Israel's appeal and God's move to meet it reveal a state which nullifies all chance of change. The desire for change is not there, and the ability to accept a freely given change is not there either. How can continued corruption, wickedness, false dealing, thievery, banditry, and the like produce either the will for change or the state of mind that would welcome it? The impasse in which God finds himself becomes frighteningly clear. The situation apparently is intolerable since any solution is impossible. The further God goes to meet his lost people, the further they retreat; the more he offers restoration, the more they refuse it. The very offering of love seems only to make matters worse.

God's clear-sighted understanding of the impasse in 7:1 is matched with Israel's contrasting blindness in v. 2. One is almost tempted to agree with the observation that "where ignorance is bliss 'tis folly to be wise." God is burdened with wisdom. He remembers all their evil words in the past, and their present villainy is even now before his face. Caught in the trap of his own love for Israel, his omniscience only makes matters worse. As for Israel, "they do not consider" even though "their deeds encompass them." They do not remember, and they cannot see. They are deficient in everything: in all virtue and in all true devotion, and now they are shown to be blind. Yet it is God who laments, not Israel. Thus contrasts and paradoxes mount. God, in offering to restore Israel and heal them, conveniently forgets, so to speak, that they are incapable of accepting. Now the same God remembers all. Israel is surrounded by incontrovertible evidence and proof, yet they are totally unaware and, apparently, content with things as they are. This blithe spirit romps down the road to ruin, not having understood the fundamental fact of their faith—that heaven and earth are one, and religion and behavior are inseparable.

7:3-7   The second part of the poem (vv. 3-7) lowers our eyes to show us further evidence of how faithless Israel lives. Two sets of images are brought together: a corrupt and conspiring court and a stifling baker's kitchen. Although these images are not normally associated, in this instance they marry effectively to give a picture of the heat and horrors of palace intrigue. Two questions then arise concerning context. First, are we in the realm of the general, or is this a particular conspiracy that is mentioned here? I would opt for the latter. Kings were coming and going very quickly during Hosea's time — three were murdered (Zechariah, Shallum, and Pekahiah) between the years 745 and 737 B.C. There is a strong chance that these verses emerge from this period or a little later, perhaps 733. The second question concerns content. Are we dealing with an impressionistic account of how things tended to be— drinking parties far into the night with debauchery the order of the day and sudden death not unknown—or is this a tale about a certain group of crafty courtiers and a mysterious baker (who appears twice, vv. 4b and 6b) who are engaged in killing the king once they have got him drunk? I again opt for the latter. A tale seems to underlie the passage, but poetic form has made it more impressionistic and, therefore, more available to succeeding centuries. There is, therefore, a certain ambivalence in any interpretation. How, for example, do we interpret the word "they"? Verses 3 and 6 in the RSV suggest that we are dealing with a specific group. Other translations make such an understanding unavoidable. For example, v. 5a has been translated "By day they made our king ill," and v. 6 can be read "When they drew near, their heart was like an oven. During their ambush all night long their baker slept until morning." We must, therefore, include two and possibly three levels of understanding in our exposition. These verses were originally concerned with a group who plotted successfully to murder their king, possibly helped by a compliant baker who overslept. However, we have received the story not in its original setting but in the context of God's word of judgment and mercy to Israel. In the new context its meaning has been extended and has become something typical and symbolic. It is now about a people and its politics, in particular about how that people has treated another of God's great gifts—the gift of kingship. At yet another level of understanding an old yarn has become a cautionary tale that is able to carry God's word into the midst of any political institution.

The king is shown to be corrupt because he is pleased by corruption (v. 3). An existing weakness of his is played upon, magnified, and taken advantage of—a weakness shared by the inner ring of the powerful. The plotter had an easy task, as the defense had already been breached by the monarch's own personal vice. The images begin to pile upon each other. Whatever was the role of the baker in the previous version, it has changed considerably as he and his fires and ovens combine with wine, adultery, and treachery to complete a picture of license and orgy that becomes more and more shameful and out of control. As the revels proceed revolution becomes simple; the king "stretches out his hand with the mockers" as though he himself were joining the conspirators and abetting his own destruction. The oven image dominates. The heat spreads to everything, temperatures rise, passions inflame; anger which had been smouldering now bursts forth and becomes a blazing fire that burns up the ruler, and before long will consume the kingdom.

If we are correct in assuming that the raw material of the verses was an account of the assassination of one of Israel's kings and that later this was transposed into a more general warning and counsel about kingship, then the correctness of the assumption is further confirmed by the last sentence of v. 7: "All their kings have fallen; and none of them calls upon me." Obviously this is not part of the original story. It must follow after the deaths of several kings, a sufficient number to warrant the use of "all." The phrase "none of them" similarly is being used to extend the application of the incident which has now become typical.

What then are the points which are being stressed? Much depends first on how we view Hosea's concept of kingship and whether these verses are in accord with it or not, and second on how we understand the use of the third person plural pronoun throughout and the first person plural "our" in v. 5a. We must assume that Hosea was a man of his time even though a highly critical one, and that he therefore accepted kingship as normal and the Israelite kings as gifts from God within the Covenant. His protests and objections (cf. 8:4) were, once more, against the abuse of kingship and not against its proper use, much the same as his criticisms of sacrifice which were not against sacrifice as such. The acceptance of kingship as being of the essence of Israel's existence is implied in the expression "our king" in 7:5a. With all his imperfections he was their king; ideally he was God's appointee and the people owed him their loyalty. Where then lies the cause for protest? The clue is in the use of "their" and "them." God the kingmaker has been dethroned to make way for earthly kingmakers. Kings are now made by "them," and whether the "them" refers to a plotting, treasonous clique or to Israel as a whole is not the main point at issue. The heart of the problem is that things have gotten out of hand and the government has been removed from God's hands. Secularization has taken over, and the secularism of Israel's life follows in its train. Removed from his due worship at his shrines, it was only a matter of time before all other authority was removed from him and alien ideologies began to determine the policies of state and control the political processes. But the removal of authorities was only apparent. The secularist's writ did not run as they imagined it did. Despite all appearances God was still in charge. Therefore "their" kings have fallen (v. 7).

The above understanding receives support from the final phrase, "and none of them calls upon me." Whether the "them" is the group of assassins or the whole people that tolerate such behavior is now secondary. Two other matters have priority.

1. To call upon God is what one does in a lament. Thus this final phrase is underlining yet another of the contrasts that exist between God's dealings with Israel and Israel's life before God. Israel's life before God, as we see in the Psalms, is intended to move between the poles of praise and lament. In good times they should turn to God in praise and thanksgiving; in the evil day they can, with confidence, cry unto the LORD and he will hear and heal. This final statement in v. 7 is a clear accusation that lamenting has ceased. Israel even in extremity does not cry "out of the depths." This is the direct opposite of God's actions. The chapter commences with God's lament. He has no need to lament and cry out, for he humbles himself to share Israel's sorrow and suffering. The people of Israel, with every reason to avail themselves of the mercy of God and to cry to him, do nothing of the sort.

2. Why is it that none of them calls upon God? Surely not because they are atheists. Theirs was a time of great religiosity and devotional zeal; faith was actually fashionable. Also it was hardly likely that they were too proud to receive help; they were already seeking many kinds of help at the shrines in all sorts of bizarre ways. Is not the cause the one already referred to: secularization? Since the time of Solomon or perhaps even David, there had been a tendency to leave certain areas of life to God, and other areas to the gods; still others the people sought to retain within their own hands. One of these was the whole political sphere. This for some had become a walled garden, independent of God's estate. It was an autonomous region that they thought they could look after themselves; God had plenty to do in other areas. Consequently if things went wrong in politics one did not go crying to God about it. This was not a religious matter. It belonged to the real world and was an issue to be taken care of by real people with their feet on the ground.

If this view is correct, we see in the passage what happens when politics becomes an autonomous region divorced from God's law. Politics does not become irreligious; rather, it becomes a surrogate religion moving out of the orbit of God's law and establishing its own norms and absolutes, which are assumed to be beyond criticism and judgment. In the Torah the social, political, and cultural laws are one and indivisible, and all draw their meaning, power, and judgment from the worship of the one God at the one altar. Hosea might be seen as giving us a satire on the new religion — the worship of politics with its pseudo-procedures, pseudo-emotions, and pseudo-kings. Its rituals take place in a pseudo-temple; in the true temple there is fire and smoke and incense and sacrifice presided over by alert priests. This new surrogate religion is not lacking in such things. There is heat and smoke and fire, but these belong to the kitchen whose high priest, the baker, cannot keep awake! And in place of the scent of incense which should waft worshippers to holiness there are the fumes of wine which drive people to evil. And the sacrifice is the king who is led willingly to his slaughter. The zeal of this new political house is eating them all up, beginning with its kings.

7:8-12   These verses remain within the political realm but move on into the area of external affairs. Verse 8 tells of Ephraim, the northern tribes of Israel, mixing "with the peoples"; v. 9 tells of aliens who "devour his strength," and v. 11 specifies Egypt and Assyria as two (no doubt the main two) countries involved. The change of subject in v. 8 is clear, and yet the continuities are even clearer. They include the interdependence of religious faith and "worldly" existence; Israel's rebellion and futile attempt to live without God; their refusal to return; their blindness and stupidity; their loss of identity; God as their loving destroyer yet still lamenting. There is even continuity with the kitchen metaphor in v. 8 and possibly in v. 9. Some commentators believe that the verses belong to the period of the Syro-Ephraimitic war and should be dated at 733 B.C. along with everything from 5:8 onwards. Whether this is correct or not, the original context was certainly one of uncertainty and vacillation in which Israel's main concern was for survival at any cost.

Ephraim is clearly the object of the original attack, receiving a double mention in v. 8. The baking theme also appears twice in this verse: the obvious reference in the second half of the cake "not turned" and the use of the verb "to mix," which is a cooking term. Both images permit varied interpretations. The mixing image may be nothing more than an additional blow against Ephraim's state of confusion as it feebly struggles in the dangerous whirlpool of international chicanery. I prefer another possibility which takes seriously the reflexive form of the verb. Ephraim was not only a crazy mixed-up country (which it undoubtedly was); it had brought that condition upon itself and had deliberately mixed itself in with the nations. Much here is at stake. Israel's place was not intended to be among the nations (Num. 23:9). It was to be a people apart, belonging to God, a peculiar people in every sense. Yet Israel had deliberately repudiated this peculiarity and chosen to associate itself with the nations. A rejection of identity is implied: a deliberate choosing of a forbidden way—in fact, not just any forbidden way, but the most prohibited way of all. The choice of an identity among the nations rather than the identity given by God through election was equivalent to idolatry or, to use Hosea's language, equivalent to harlotry, because alignment with the nations involved the accepting of their gods and a loosening of Israel's hold on the living God.

Furthermore, such mixing with the nations also implies what was made explicit in Hos. 7:3-7: politics had been taken out of God's hands and had been made secular. It was none of God's business what went on in this independent "nonreligious" realm, and if Israel chose to trust the nations for survival rather than God, then that was Israel's business—or, at least, so they imagined. The decision to mix had at least one other outcome, but as it is central to one of Hosea's main teachings we shall leave it for later discussion.

To put their faith in the nations rather than in God draws forth the appropriate comment that Ephraim is half-baked. Cakes in those days were placed close to the inside wall of the oven, and when one side was brown the cake was turned over so that the other side could be baked. Ephraim was still unturned, declares Hosea, and therefore burned on one side and raw on the other. It is the same picture as we found in vv. 3-7: immaturity combined with excessive heat that burns immoderately. The verb here is different, but it is not impossible that a link with the constant demand that Ephraim "turn and return" is intended. But an Ephraim who can be insane enough to choose Egypt and Assyria rather than God is destined always to be on the wrong side.

Verse 9 takes up the point about stupidity, joining it to ignorance on an heroic scale. For incredibly Ephraim chooses the alien nations even though the aliens have proved their hostility by devouring Ephraim's strength. The Ephraimites have been blind to the changes from the outside; they are equally unaware of the internal weakening. They are getting old, and either can't or won't admit it. Or it is possible that the white hairs are the white hairs of mold? If so, this would fit with the cake metaphor—the nation is half-baked and moldy but doesn't know it. Such darkness of mind! How can any people which doesn't know its own age know God?

Stupid and blind, Ephraim is still proud, and their pride witnesses against them. Verse 10 begins with a reference to 5:5a; it is possible, moreover, that the whole of 7:10 is not original (cf. the Jerusalem Bible). If indeed the verse is a later addition, one could consider it as all the more important in consequence. The contents of this verse are not novel. Verse 10a is a quotation, and 10b and c are so central to Hosea that they sound here almost like a refrain (cf. 4:6-12).

This part of the poem (7:8-12) ends with two verses (11 and 12) that obviously belong together because the first likens Ephraim to a bird and the second depicts God as the fowler. Verse 11 is very similar to v. 8. They both speak of two subjects: Ephraim's identification with the nations and the nation's moronic nature. Ephraim is like a dove, but this is not intended as a compliment. A dove flies hither and thither, uncertain and indecisive. What is more, it is "heartless," which in this context is equivalent to "brainless" and says nothing about lack of compassion or sympathy. The immediate reasons for being so castigated are Ephraim's reliance upon the great powers and then not being able to make up their mind which of these powers offered the best insurance against destruction. Verse 12 continues to show us the situation from God's point of view. From Ephraim's standpoint, of course, things are very different. They undoubtedly see themselves as dealing with the real world uncomplicated by the mysterious but irrelevant world of the preachers. As they see it, they are making a reasonable assessment of the evidence and are deciding responsibly for the greater benefit of the nation. The reality is very different. They are infantile, blind, ignorant, and hopeless. Ephraim's leaders are not courageous statesmen but panicking birds about to be netted by the God they thought they had made redundant. As always the fundamental problem is the theological one. How is life in this world seen? If God is otiose or pensionable, or even absent, then the great factors in our immediate environment—the factors that demand immediate and constant attention, the factors round which all else must revolve—are of course the Egypts and the Assyrias, the great powers of our day too. But if God is who and what he and Hosea say he is, then the Egyptians and Assyrians are pawns in a chess game that is invisible to all but those who listen to Hosea and the few with him who prophesy. If God is known, then Egypt and Assyria are opportunities for obedience or disobedience within an immeasurably greater reality. If they and the other nations and their ambitions, plots, and fears are thought to be the reality, then such a "theology" can only land one trapped and pinioned in God's net.

7:13-16   These verses conclude a series of oracles which may have begun at 5:8. They also bring to a close the second section of the book which began at ch. 5. The themes follow on from what has gone before but move to a pessimistic climax in which Israel is once more being derided for turning to Egypt. Before we look at individual verses, therefore, let us examine how at least five of the themes are partially rounded off in this passage.

1. Israel has sought security in alliances rather than in God. The people have vacillated between Assyria and Egypt, assuming that they have a choice of options in their struggle for survival. Hosea 7:16 says that they sought and found what they were looking for —in fact, they had actually got what they wanted. They had turned to Egypt, but instead of finding security there, had lost it and found themselves once more in bondage. Surely this was "poetic justice."

2. The theme of the God of the Exodus versus the gods of Canaan is very clearly present in these verses. Israel chose the gods of Canaan, and they now find themselves driven from Canaan and sent back to Egypt. More poetic justice.

3. God had redeemed Israel by bringing them out of Egypt, but Israel had rejected God and his redemption. So God reverses what had happened and puts Israel back in Egypt.

4. Israel, chosen from out of all the nations to be God's peculiar people, has chosen its own destiny among the nations. God's response is to accept that decision, and like a taut bow throw Israel back among the nations.

5. In season and out of season God has been promising disaster to his people. Now the disaster has fallen, and Israel is derided in the land of Egypt!

We have seen how this section moves towards a conclusion of punishment and destruction. It is as though the Exodus had never happened. Pharaoh had proved victorious. But Egypt is not just any country. It is the biblical land of ambivalence, a land of bondage but also a land where refugees flee in times of hunger and anger. For even in Egypt there is a glimmer of hope.

The four verses are a lament over the rebellions and a dirge over the doomed. They begin with a cry of woe and end with the sentence of punishment. Verses 13 and 15 are similar as they contrast yet again the behavior of God and the behavior of his people. Israel strays, Israel wanders, but still God is the redeeming God. Under the old covenant God must pronounce woe and devastation, but the urge to redeem remains. The redeeming work, however, cannot proceed because "they speak lies against me." The word "redeem" takes us back to the Exodus (Exod. 15:13), where a parallel word is used. Presumably these "lies" denied God's power to redeem, for if the people had begun to believe their own lies and had therefore ceased to look to God, then obviously they would look elsewhere for security and redemption. This is what had happened, and Israel now trusted in the gods of Canaan and of the nations. When they did lament and cry to God (Hos. 7:14) or confess (6:1-3), it was not "from the heart." At times they were not incapable of crying to God, but when they did it was wrong in at least three respects. First, they were so steeped in the local beliefs and practices that they treated Yahweh as they would the Baals—with wailing upon beds (whatever that signifies) and with the self-mutilation (cf. 1 Kgs. 18:28) which was common local practice. Second, their motivation was suspect; their appeal was merely a form of "cupboard love." They approached God only when the cupboard was bare and tried to turn him into the agricultural god which he was in their imagination. Third, for rebels all is rebellious. Their very prayer to God becomes an extension of their life of disobedience.

Hosea 7:15, like v. 13, reminds us of the Exodus. There God had strengthened his people and redeemed them. In v. 13 the response is one of lies and lack of belief in his redeeming power; in v. 15 the lies and unbelief have engendered evil plotting or, as one translation suggests, they even treated him as the evil one. All this can only have one result: the rejected God will reject and destroy his people. At v. 14 they had appealed, so now they return; but if the appeal was valueless, the return is even more so, because instead of returning to God they turn to Baal! A Baal-orientated Israel can only be rejected.

The whole purpose in choosing Israel had been for mission. They were to be the light to the nations, the agent who, because of their own orientation to God, would one day be instrumental in turning all nations to him. They were God's weapon against all evil things, especially against wrong beliefs and wrong worship which led people into wrong ways of living. Now the weapon was injuring the user. It had become worse than useless, it was even a question of fighting for the enemy. Therefore the bow must be cast away. In contrast with the time of the Exodus when God had trained and strengthened Israel's arms, Israel's arms shall now fail: "their princes shall fall by the sword because of the insolence of their tongue." The mouth and the spoken word are very important to Hosea (cf. v. 14a). In the present four verses the people "speak lies," "cry," "wail," and "devise evil"—presumably in conversation. All the speaking, crying, wailing, and plotting reveals what is in their innermost hearts. Hearts full of insolence to God merit the just reward of derision in Egypt.

The life of the nation is a theological matter first and foremost. In ch. 7 all the major departments of Israel's life are touched upon and condemned or threatened: public morality and social affairs in v. 1; the court and political matters generally in vv. 3-7; national pride, intelligence, fortitude, and international affairs in vv. 8-12; religious observance, military matters, the country's future, security, and survival, not to mention its honor in vv. 13-16. All are judged and found wanting, and the want is theological in nature. Their "God-talk" is all wrong and inevitably everything else goes wrong as a result. The real king, God, is dethroned, and the would-be "kings" scramble to take his seat: the earthly kings and king-makers; nature and the gods of nature; food and drink; political ideology and political passion; the nation and its existence. Each one of them makes a bid to sit "high and lifted up" and claim the right to be called the holy one of Israel. Each one would become the absolute, the final arbiter owing no wider allegiance and becoming determinative of all other allegiances. The effect is a chaos that can only deserve destruction. There is only one possibility for Israel (and ultimately for any other country or culture) that God is still enthroned. If the living God is not on the throne, that throne is never empty; it is always occupied. And once installed upon it, even the best of creatures becomes the abomination of desolation when it apes the Creator. Ultimate loyalty must necessarily be ex-

93

tended to something or somebody. The so-called atheist is a verbal creation and nothing more. Something will always claim, and successfully claim, the right to make other loyalties secondary; but only one can do this without disaster ensuing, and that is God. Israel moves to disaster because their relativities had become absolutes and the true Absolute had been judged and supposedly found wanting.

Lament figures prominently in this chapter. God laments in the first and fourth parts and Israel laments, albeit falsely, in v. 14. To believe in the God of Israel is, at times, to lament. Part of Israel's tragedy in Hosea's time is the inability properly to lament—to lament for their sins and to come with tears and lamentations to the all-merciful God who longs to heal and save. Israel's inability or refusal truly to lament is an integral part of their rebellion and their inability to accept the gift of redemption. God is distinguished most of all by his nature as Redeemer. In his inner dialogues and dilemmas it is always his will to redeem which eventually triumphs. In the OT this is demonstrated not so much in doctrines as in actual manifestations of his redemptive powers at work — God's saving acts of which many are recorded; but there is one alone that stands in the central place: the Exodus. An impressive feature of God's saving acts and of their narration in the OT is that frequently the record of what God does to save includes the account of Israel's cry to God, whereupon it is in response to this lamenting cry that God acts to save (cf. Deut. 26; Exod. 3:7-9). The humble, loving, noncoercing God not only saves in response to a genuine cry for help; it is as though that cry has a necessary place in God's redeeming work. Mankind's need, their recognition of that need, and its articulation almost become part of the saving work. The Christian reader of Hosea can never forget that in that most sacred moment when the world was being redeemed our LORD cried out the words of an OT lament: "My God, my God, why hast thou forsaken me"?

SECTION III
THE SPIRITUAL HISTORY OF ISRAEL

OF KINGS AND CULT
Hosea 8:1-14

The division of the book into four sections is not without a little arbitrariness, which is most apparent in relation to ch. 8. By the time one reaches ch. 11 the determination of this third division and the justification for its title, "The Spiritual History of Israel," are quite clear; but in the present chapter the continuity with Section II is so obvious that it is legitimate to question whether the sectional boundary is precisely between chs. 7 and 8. For example, kingship and cult are not new. Assyria and Egypt already played an important part in the previous chapter, and 8:1a is almost an echo of 5:8. Nevertheless the division is warranted on at least two grounds. Most verses in ch. 8 do in fact have a backward look into Israel's past (e.g., vv. 1, 3, 4, 5), finding there evidence for God's revealing or Israel's spurning. The second ground is that where there is an obvious dependence upon and continuity with what has gone before, the later expression is far from being a carbon copy. Usually a considerable development is noticeable. For example, the chapter's two main topics of kings and cult are advanced a good deal further than before: kingship is discussed in vv. 4 and 10, the cult in vv. 4-6 and 11-13.

As before, our question will be more theological than historical, but this does not deny all importance to historical questions and answers. The theological and canonical interests are not independent of other viewpoints: on the contrary, they need to be considered from every possible angle and, where necessary, built upon along with whatever foundation other approaches can contribute. What can historians say about ch. 8? A good case can be made out for maintaining that the whole of ch. 8 originated from the same period as in 5:8–7:16. The similarity of 8:1 and 5:8 (and several other verses in the two contexts) suggests that they both belong to a period of military and political turmoil and that, indeed, it is the same period. We can therefore assign the two passages to 733 B.C. or perhaps a little more than ten years previous. Hans Walter Wolff makes a good case for 733 and argues that the setting of the address (or addresses) was in Samaria, where "a gathering of people may have presented the opportunity for Hosea to dispute with the leading circles of the royal residence, similar to 5:1" (*Hosea*, 137).

The historical similarities that exist within both sections (chs. 4-7 and 8-11) are paralleled by literary similarities, especially in chs. 7 and 8. Chapter 7 has been likened to a sandwich in which the beginning and the end are covenantal (dealing with the vertical relationship between Israel and God), while in between are particular examples of horizontal earthly matters where Israel's behavior jeopardizes the covenant. Chapter 8 begins with the clear statement that "they have broken my covenant, and transgressed my law." This is then followed by a list of instances specifying how Israel's conduct has broken the covenant and transgressed the law. In a modified sense the "Covenantal Sandwich" is still preserved because 8:14 begins with the vertical declaration that "Israel has forgotten his Maker." A further similarity in the form of the two chapters is that a return to Egypt is referred to in both conclusions (7:16 and 8:13).

The behavioral content of ch. 8 has been analyzed in a variety of ways. As the title of this chapter indicates, most of the content is related to the twin themes of king and cult. A more detailed analysis produces six subsections:

1. A new king is installed without God's approval (v. 4a);

2. Idols are made and their worship is destructive (v. 4b);

3. Samaria worships the calf (or the bull): a do-it-yourself parody of the true worship, which ends in destruction (vv. 5-6);

4. Israel has chosen to buy security from Assyria, with the result that they have become lost among the nations;

5. A sacrificial system has evolved which is powered by lust and has therefore become an occasion for sin rather than an opportunity for forgiveness;

6. Palaces and fortified cities have multiplied, making Israel forget their Maker.

8:1-3 Wherever in the chapter there is any indication as to who is the speaker it points to God himself. If these verses are a divine speech, then who is being addressed? Is God speaking to the prophet as watchman, or is God through the prophet addressing the watchman-herald? Conscious that behind the present opaqueness there lies a distinct historical event, we must recognize that its outlines are blurred—perhaps deliberately—so that God through this prophecy is addressing later generations of Israel as well. The new chapter and the new section begin with an emphasized warning. The promised disaster, as punishment for apostasy, is drawing nearer. A vulture is hovering overhead, ready to swoop. The house of the LORD, which can mean the Promised Land where Israel dwells, is in imminent danger. Already the smell of death is upon it; the vulture recognizes a ready victim. The house of the LORD is no longer protected by the LORD—in fact, precisely the opposite. Whether the vulture is God or merely an agent of God is immaterial. The question is the same. God is the enemy. This chapter is harsher in some ways than previous ones. There is, for example, no call to Israel to return. The only return in it is return to Egypt! The only sign of hope in the first three verses, or indeed in the whole of the chapter, is the sign of the trumpet—yet we don't actually hear that it was ever blown. Nevertheless, it is there as a symbol. The vulture is still above. The victim may be near to death but is still breathing. Maybe there is still a possibility of escape if the trumpet is blown. Surely there is hope, because it is the God who has summoned the vulture who is also urging the trumpeter to blow. The dilemma and dialogue which exist in God himself are once more observable.

The explanation of the vulture and the warning trumpet appear in the same verse (v. 1). Israel has broken "my covenant" and transgressed "my law." The Hebrew words used are *berit* and *torah;* and almost certainly, given the rest of the book of Hosea, they are to be read in the context of the Exodus. The making of the covenant (Exod. 19–24) includes within the ratification ceremony the giving of the Ten Commandments and other basic laws (Exod. 20–23). In that setting the *torah* is presented almost as the conditions which had to be accepted before the *berit* could be ratified. Undoubtedly this conditionality was one aspect of the relationship existing between the two, but it wasn't the whole story. The covenant was a conditional covenant in some ways, but it was even more a covenant of grace in others. It wasn't obedience to the *torah* which made the *berit* possible in the first place; the *berit* was a gift. But like any gift the *berit* had to be accepted and cherished, and the *torah* offered the instructions that went with the gift. Everything freely given has to be freely received and freely cared for. A car may be a free gift, but it has to be insured, and taxed, and serviced, and cleaned if it is to remain usable. The torah provided the directions that were included with the *berit* for preserving it and all that went with it. The two belonged indissolubly together, just as they are presented here in this poetic couplet. To break the covenant is to transgress the law and vice versa.

The personal pronoun is stressed. God speaks of "my covenant" and "my law." The implications of the "my" are numerous. The covenant and the law do not come from the Baals, nor the "kings," but from God. Nature and politics are neither outside the law and the covenant nor are they above them; they are subject to them both. The double "my" also prepares us for the "me" and the "thee" in v. 2, but most likely the pronoun is there primarily to stress the enormity of Israel's failings. The covenant has bound little, frail Israel to the land of promise. They are united with it as wife to husband and son to father. Israel's existence and identity are dependent on their relationship with God as set forth in the covenant. Without it they are nothing; they don't even exist. They are merely a rabble of slaves; they are not even the nation, just like other nations, which they are anxious to become. The "my" underlies the insanity of Israel's rebellion. It is yet another and powerful way of referring to their death wish and impending suicide.

God's inner dialogue is further shared with the unspecified audience. The trumpet with its suggestion of hope is followed by another hopeful sign: Israel laments. The cry that might be the turning point leading to return and salvation does indeed come, and like the confession in 6:1-3 it comes with all the appearance of adequacy. It is made to God and not to the Baals—to the God of the covenant and of the law—and it is made in precisely the right terms. Israel had discerned what was the central problem: the knowledge of God. This it is claimed is not absent: "My God, we Israel know thee." This knowledge of God was knowledge of the God who had revealed himself at the Exodus. It was not just intellectual knowledge or conceptual wisdom; it was the knowledge that comes from a close relationship and which could do nothing to impair that relationship. It was knowledge which implied covenant keeping and which made impossible any breaking of the law; and of course herein lies the explanation of God's angry response. What could be more outrageous than to demonstrate in every way possible that Israel had broken covenant and transgressed the law and then have the impertinence to make a show of virtue by pretending exactly the opposite? It was more than a lie, uttered away beyond insensitivity and hypocrisy; it was a Judas kiss and was recognized as such. The divine dialogue comes to one of its temporary conclusions in v. 3.

There is to be no respite. Sentence has been passed and is about to be executed: "the enemy shall pursue him." The trumpet may still sound, but it will achieve nothing. The time of warning and of second chances is past. The hawks and doves in God's "parliament" have ended their debate with a clear win by the hawks and their champion the vulture. Israel's future is in the talons of the bird of prey. The final decision comes about because "Israel has spurned the good." No narrow definition can be given to the word "good," nor is one needed. It is obviously a "postmortem" term signifying all that is not bad. Therefore the whole expression includes covenant breaking and transgressing the law as well as the blatant perjury of falsely claiming to know God. It includes all the sins that have already been spelled out and those yet to come. But "good" is not only a generic name for a long list of virtues; "good" is God himself! In breaking the covenant and transgressing the law, in worshipping the Baals and cutting politics off from the life of faith, in sham confession and lying lament, they were doing but one thing: they were spurning God himself. God's response of sending the vulture-enemy was then not vengeance or hatred or peevishness; his action was demanded by the covenant in that it called for both blessing and curse (Deut. 27–28). To spurn God was to close the only possible door to blessing and to opt for the curse.

8:4-7   So far in this chapter the accusations have been of a general nature — breaking the covenant, transgressing the law, spurning the good. Now follows the more detailed evidence, which we have already divided into six parts. Hosea 8:4 introduces two out of the six — autonomous king-making and idol worship. As well as being examples of Israel's disobedience, these two are also representative of the two main categories into which that disobedience can be divided. If we can name the two "state and church" or "piety and politics," we cover the first five out of Israel's six errors. If, however, we prefer "culture and cult," then all six can shelter under the one heading.

Verse 4a, b takes us back to the first half of ch. 7, where king-making by foul means is described in some detail. Perhaps the earlier detail in ch. 7 is relied upon and taken for granted, because here in ch. 8 the writer is content to generalize about how kings rise and fall. In 8:4c he similarly generalizes about idol-making; but in this case, not having some previous detail to depend upon, he has to provide it in the succeeding verses (vv. 5-6). We live at the intersection of the horizontal and the vertical; the so-called material and spiritual. We belong to both because they belong together. We live in two kingdoms and are only living truly when the king of the earthly kingdom is ruling in the same manner as the heavenly king. Such was Israel's ideal. The first two commandments were designed to see that Yahweh and only Yahweh was recognized as king of the heavenly realm. This was balanced in the earthly sphere by ensuring that the *torah* ruled and that among the administrators of the *torah* were the earthly kings who were God's appointed. The appointing was done either by the bestowal of charismatic gifts appropriate to kingship or by the intervention of a prophet. Israel's rebellion according to Hosea involved an attempt to take over both kingdoms, to dethrone the rightful rulers (God and his chosen king) and install those who were amenable to Israel's wishes and in accord with Israel's desires. Israel did not desire a ruler who made absolute demands and appointed his agents to carry them out or who saw that judgment was made and punishment executed if his will was flouted. Israel wanted no external will and no external judge. The rulers they wanted in both kingdoms were intended to be their agents who carried out their wishes. Gods and kings were to be made in Israel's image to suit Israel's purposes. The people wanted, and were in favor of getting, made-to-measure gods and kings who would not impose an external will but would happily be imposed upon, who would not measure Israel and find them wanting but who would accommodate themselves to Israel's measurements.

Verse 4 describes the process of creating man-made kings and gods. The divinely-appointed procedures for choosing the rulers are bypassed, and the God-substitutes are fashioned out of silver and gold. The description of the process is given in full, right up to its ultimate conclusion, which is destruction. Here is the ultimate irony, the final illusion. A process which is designed to please, to prosper, to provide security, satisfaction, food, fertility, and survival ends in destruction. The made-to-measure gods do not fit the realities of the situation, and they measure nothing. It is they who are measured and found to be vanities which bring only death.

Some details of the false gods are now presented, and where better to begin than with the most famous graven image in northern Israel, "the calf of Samaria"? Here I am assuming that Hosea is speaking of the idol which Jeroboam I placed in Bethel (1 Kgs. 12:28ff.). There is no evidence that such an idol ever stood in the city of Samaria, whereas there is plenty of evidence that the "calf" in Bethel was worshipped down to the time of Hosea (2 Kgs. 10:29; 14:24; 15:9, 18, 24, 28). The expression "calf of Samaria" is therefore already symbolic and is not limited to a specific image in one specific place. Samaria stands for the country as a whole, and the calf indicates the idolatrous worship which is centered in the royal sanctuary (cf. Amos 7:13). The whole of the nation's worship is being condemned as leading away from God and not leading to him. It has become its own opposite. Designed to keep the covenant relationship wholesome, it ensures its destruction. Intended to flow naturally from the law, it transgresses the fundamental tenets of the law. God has no alternative. He must, with burning anger, reject the cult. Israel, in their apostasy, has spurned the good. God in anguished justice must spurn one of the major manifestations of that apostasy: "the calf of Samaria." That the anger and the spurning are not done lightly is shown clearly in the second half of Hos. 8:5. God's reluctance to spurn Israel and his continued longing over them immediately appears in the lamenting language of the first couplet: "How long will it be till they are pure in Israel?" or "How long will they be incapable of innocence?"

The dialogue in God's heart never seems to cease. Condemnation brings out lament as love and judgment do battle. The lament and longing hold the stage for a moment and then, as though God were afraid that love would overwhelm justice, the cause of justice is fed by more thoughts about the idol. "A workman made it; it is not God." God's burning anger is further fulfilled by these thoughts and their articulation, and love is stilled. The judge's sentence is pronounced: "The calf of Samaria shall be broken in pieces." The first half of v. 6 is not only one of the earliest statements about idols in the OT; it is also one of the most enlighten-

ing. The words are spoken in great indignation and deserve ex-
clamation marks. The wrath is obvious; there may also be considerable sarcasm. The first phrase, "A workman made it" or "An expert made it," could almost be a quotation from the advertising
material of the idol-makers: a salesman's boast. "This is no common or garden image, nor an apprentice's work. This was made by
our top carver." If so it is now pronounced upon furiously and
scathingly. The bitterness bites: "An expert made it, indeed." A
god, even a god made by an expert, is a contradiction in terms. A
made god is, by definition, not a god. God makes; he creates; he
is not made. This calf of Samaria which has broken the covenant
and transgressed the law shall justly and appropriately be broken in
pieces.

Did the people of Samaria think of the calf in a representative
way, a symbol that stood for something outside and greater than
itself? If so, what? If it symbolizes the Baals or fertility, then the
violent rejection is understandable; but two questions remain.
First, what if it represented Yahweh? Perhaps this was even more
horrifying. Yahweh was the incomparable God and therefore could
not be represented. He was also the utterly free, not to be tied
down or limited. He disposed and was at no one's disposal. He
moved and supported and carried his people. How could he be
moved and be supported and carried as an idol must be? The
second question looks not so much at what was being represented
as to the nature of the representation. Was it possible for the
prophets—and perhaps for Israel as a whole—even to imagine that
the graven image was only representative? We take it for granted
that an idol worshipper is always looking beyond the idol to the
"deity" it signifies and to which it points. But what if that idea
never entered into the minds of the prophets or their hearers? What
if they saw nothing but the wood or metal of the idol and believed
that they were what was being worshipped? Certainly the language
of Hosea (and of the other prophets) would support this view.

In Amos 3:3-8 the writer strengthens his argument in an unusual way. He lists many examples of how certain results follow in-
exorably from a previous combination of circumstances, and one
assumes that he is affirming a general principle or law; in that case
it is the law of cause and effect. Hosea seems to use Hos. 8:7 in a
somewhat similar manner, the differences being (1) that he utilizes
proverbial sayings to underline the principles his discourse relies

upon, and (2) that he goes beyond a simple relationship of cause and effect to an effect which is totally disproportionate.

Admitting that humility is required with regard to both the translation and the interpretation of the verses, and accepting the RSV translation as a good and possible one, then the verse relates to the rest of the chapter as follows: Israel has manufactured both gods and kings. This is their sowing, and it is a sowing of vanity and nothingness. But it does not end in vanity. Vanity does not just produce more vanity, and wind does not just cause wind. When one sows one sows to multiply; that is what agriculture is all about. So winds do not just produce harvests of wind; they cause whirlwinds. Israel's sowing of their made-to-measure gods and kings would not end there or merely produce a few more similar gods and kings. There would be growth, terrifying cancerous growth, and an awesome harvest. Winds would become whirlwinds. Israel's apostasy would become utter, total disaster.

The principle is clearest in the first couplet, but it is also present in the other two. In every case the end is worse than the beginning. As wind becomes whirlwind so standing grain becomes "no meal," and a possible harvest only nourishes the enemy. Thus, each time the disproportionate yield is emphasized, Israel's deeds are seen as seeds, and these are planted in God's soil which in this instance is horrifyingly fertile. In the human sphere an eye for an eye and a tooth for a tooth may suffice. Where mankind is bound by covenant to God another law is at work in human history, and it is not a law of simple retribution or just proportion. Sometimes it results in immeasurable unreasonable blessing; at other times mankind's breeze becomes a typhoon.

8:8-10   The principle of the unwelcome harvest is now related to the political sphere, and the intended connection is made clear in the first verb, "swallow." Verse 7 ends with aliens devouring (or "swallowing") the harvest; v. 8 begins with Israel being swallowed up. The main subject is one already touched upon in 7:8, 9, 16: Israel's absorption among the nations. In ch. 8 it is developed a little more and possibly linked to Israel's cultic failings in v. 9.

The whirlwind which will certainly strike Israel is amplified in two images in v. 8. Originally there had been no Israel, only the nations (Gen. 10); then gradually Israel emerged from the nations as the result of election (Gen. 12:1-3; Amos 3:2) and was appointed to serve God on behalf of the nations (Exod. 19:5, 6). Israel's reason for existence was to be a people apart. Their life was to be distinct, to be separate. To return to their roots and once more to be at one with the nations was a form of death wish. Now the wish had been made and granted. The nations had gobbled or would very quickly gobble Israel up, just as the aliens had already gobbled or would gobble up Israel's food. The second image expands the first. Israel's destiny was not only to be absorbed. In a sense that was what they sought: to follow the crowd, to resign from the responsibilities of their status as a peculiar people, and be like the other nations. This was their ambition and, on the surface, it was not all that unreasonable. Why shouldn't someone else have a spell of being a peculiar people and a nation of priests? Weren't they due for a holiday? But this was to ignore the wind/whirlwind principle. Wanting to be like everyone else, they harvested something very different. Instead of the identification with the nations which they thought they had chosen, they found themselves rejected by the club they wished to join. They had not become an honored member but had found themselves like a pot discarded and thrown on the scrapheap. Spurned by God, they were now spurned by the nations.

Political imagery is now pinned down with historical fact as Hos. 8:9 records an approach that Israel made to Assyria, bribe in hand. Most likely this refers to Ahaz' offering of tribute to Tiglath-pileser III in 733. The amount according to the Assyrian records was 1000 talents of silver. From Israel's point of view this was a hardheaded, reasonable, perhaps even astute, move. Israel was joining a political club which would guarantee the nation's security; naturally there was a price, and Israel was willing to pay it. Survival at that price was cheap. Once more Israel sowed the wind; soon came the whirlwind. Ephraim becomes like a wild ass, alone and solitary. The points being made are aided by a pun effective in Hebrew but not reproducible in English: the consonants of the Hebrew terms for "wild ass" and "Ephraim" are the same. This verbal similarity strengthens the identification being made. Israel is following the herd instinct by seeking to join the nations, but more than instinct is needed. Verse 8 has shown Israel thrown on the international scrapheap; now the people's isolation is stressed in two ways. The first is by the wild ass metaphor. This animal lives in herds, so "a wild ass wandering alone" is exceptional, unnatural.

The second image is the disgusting one of the unwanted harlot who can find no fee-paying customers or even lovers who will accept her embraces free of charge. It is she who has to pay men to couple with her. Israel's isolation from God and mankind seems to be complete. Seeking to be sociable, Israel reaps the whirlwind of abject loneliness. The picture of Israel's degradation is now complete. Driven by her desires, she has sought to buy religious and political favors by hiring "lovers" in both realms. Trying to escape from God and mix with the nations, she has succeeded merely in isolating herself. However, the isolation is not final because God has other plans. He will be a shepherd, but a strange one; for he will gather Israel together for further disaster. The nature of the disaster is opaque, but a little more light is found if we translate not as the RSV does but as follows: "They shall shortly writhe because of the burden of the king of princes." They have sown the wish for security; they will reap suffering, presumably because Assyria lays upon them intolerable burdens.

8:11-13   So we go from politics to piety as we move to vv. 11-13. But the drama is the same; only the scenery is different. From man-made kings and their wrongdoing to man-made gods and their misdirection, rebellion, punishment, and the contrast between God and Israel, all the continuing themes are present—all except hope. It may even be that this passage is still under the influence of v. 7 and its principles of unwelcome harvest and disproportionate reaction, as the idea of multiplication occurs at least three times. Israel multiplies altars, God multiplies his laws, and Israel multiplies fortified cities.

When the covenant was ratified at the time of Moses (Exod. 24) there was a ceremony introduced by a sacrifice on an altar. Altars and sacrifices, therefore, were not foreign to the religion of Yahweh; they were integral to it. The problem then is not the presence of altar and sacrifice. They are not prohibited; on the contrary, they are commanded from the beginning. The problem lies in the meaning attributed to them and the manner of their usage. It may be that Hosea is concerned with the actual number of altars. Maybe he believed that "few is beautiful" under all circumstances, or perhaps he was an early advocate of the movement which resulted in Deuteronomic legislation permitting only one altar (Deut. 12). This is possible but unlikely. The protest against multiplication is not against many altars but is against many sinful altars. Because they had become occasions for sin rather than opportunities for the cleansing of sins, their numbers had become a scandal. Shrines had degenerated into becoming "sacred" brothels. They were places of orgy rather than houses of prayer. They led away from righteousness and God: they had almost become substitutes for God and certainly hindered his true worship. Little wonder that their multiplication offended. Each new one did not nourish the faith; it did the opposite. Multiplying altars subtracted from any loyalty the people had left and divided mankind from God, God from mankind. Religious zeal led to death, not life.

God is still speaking aloud his inner thoughts in Hos. 8:12. In his musing, Israel's actual multiplication of altars is countered with an hypothetical multiplication by God. Should he increase the number of laws in order to neutralize the number of places of sin? The possibility is rejected even as it is made.

The altars that should support the law had become its enemy. The altars had become places of law avoidance and had so corrupted the judgments of the people and the values of their society that the people could no longer recognize the laws of God for what they were. Their made-to-measure gods, worshipped at made-to-measure altars, were now the source of all measurement. Every society and value system centers on a "sacred" from which it derives its notions of what is good and evil, proper and improper. Israel's value system, once drawn from the laws of the Holy One of Israel, now centered on the Baals, as the Baals had become their new "sacred." Evil had become their good, and when this evil people with evil values met the good laws of the good God, God seemed to them to be evil and not good. To multiply the laws therefore was useless. Like multiplied altars an increase in laws led to more sinning, not more virtue.

The first half of v. 13 has many possible translations, and it is by no means certain that the RSV translation is correct. We shall limit ourselves to the elements that are comparatively clear. The argument has shifted from altars, via God's laws, to the sacrifices that the altars exist to sustain and which the laws should control. The condemnation of the altars in v. 11 comprehends the rejection of the current mode of sacrifice and for the same reason: they have become paths away from God instead of ways to him. But there is some additional elaboration about motivation in v. 13. The

sacrifices here *(zebah)* are those in which part of the slain animal
was burnt on the altar and part was eaten by the worshippers as a
communion meal (Lev. 3; 7:11-18). It was therefore both a
religious ceremony and a barbecue, and like the communion meal
in Corinth concerning which the apostle Paul wrote, it was open
to the same abuses. The worshippers could eat to the glory of the
LORD or for their own bodily satisfaction. They could eat the flesh
for God's sake or they could so eat for their own sakes that their
bellies became their gods. Called to love God, they loved their own
flesh more, and also the cooked flesh in which they rejoiced.
Beneath the fleshly failure there were no doubt others. The people
loved the sacrifice and loved the flesh that filled them because they
assumed that the very eating automatically gave them two priceless benefits. By eating and enjoying themselves they believed they
were being forgiven for their sins and restored to full fellowship.
The eating made them guiltless but also, they were convinced, by
restoring them to fellowship with God it guaranteed them security.
It was a case, so they thought, not only of "eat, drink, and be
merry" but of "eat, drink, and be saved from sin and danger" or of
"luxuriate in full security." And it could indeed have been so. They
were meant to enjoy the sacrifice and the fellowship with one
another and their fellowship with God. Barbecues are a gift from
God. But they are such only under certain conditions; these conditions were written there in the laws which they were unable to
recognize as coming from God, even if God wrote them himself in
editions of ten thousand. These conditions were not met and therefore the sacrifices were unacceptable. Israel's delight of sacrifice
was not matched by God's.

   Then comes the "now" which precedes the verdict and sentence.
God remembers. He remembers their iniquity and will punish
their sins. In the OT and in the NT alike the act of remembering
is not something that is purely backward looking; it involves the
present and the future. In NT idiom, when we eat the bread and
drink the wine of communion in the present we do so in
remembrance of Christ until he comes again. The act of remembering the past affects both present and future. Similarly God's act
of remembering Israel's iniquity includes the inevitability of future
punishment. The punishment of return to Egypt has already been
mentioned in Hos. 7:16 and will be further clarified in historical
terms in 9:3; 11:5. The absence of the historical dimension here

forces us to a profound theological interpretation which is not difficult to ascertain, since the raw material of it lies on the surface.
The conjunction of the verb "return" and "Egypt," where "salvation" was first made known, is most potent. Israel has sought
security and survival by making gods and kings. This has been
Israel's sowing. Now comes the unwelcome harvest—disproportionate and full of irony. Similarly, any survival could have been
theirs if only they had "returned." Now they will return, no doubt
about it. But it will not be to the God of their salvation; it will be
to the place where it all began: the place of bondage. The harvest
is not one of safety but marks the end of the "saving history." Israel will return not to life but to death.

8:14   Hosea 8:14 adds a little that is new by speaking of great
buildings and about the nature of the threatened disaster. Otherwise it continues the established themes and forms a conclusion to
the chapter. It is that God remembers (v. 13) while Israel forgets.
Israel forgets their Maker and Protector and seeks safety elsewhere.
Like the builders of Babel, fear drives Israel to build and to rejoice
in their own technology. The Babel builders were at least striving
to reach heaven; Israel looks to this world and their own efforts in
it. They build palaces (or temples) where their man-made kings
and carved gods are employed to provide the protection that only
the Creator can offer. Fear also compels Israel (and this includes
Judah) to trust in the arms race and the multiplication of fortresses.
Their cities are forts. They live surrounded by visible, armed
security, yet they are totally insecure. In the words of Amos (chs.
1 and 2), Hosea prophesies destruction by fire. The principle of
winds growing into whirlwinds still holds.

UNWELCOME HARVEST

Hosea 9:1-17

Is ch. 9 a unity in any sense? It begins with reference to a place of festival and a time of festival. Is the whole chapter an account of one day at that festival? The celebration is a harvest festival, and so the chapter naturally introduces agricultural subjects such as threshing, winevats, land, and food. Some of the same agricultural imagery is present in ch. 10. Are we then to include ch. 10 in the festival narrative, or are the agricultural images accidental? Chapter 9 includes four historical references (vv. 9, 10a, c, 15). Are these the unifying element, one of the instances occurring in v. 9 as part of the account of the festival happenings, with the other three—from other days—being added to it as a gesture to thematic unity, if not geographical and temporal unity?

As so often with Hosea, the questions are clearer than the answers. We shall treat vv. 1-9 as belonging to Hosea's experience at the shrine and leave open whether anything else within chs. 9 and 10 actually belongs to the same event. It is interesting to point out that at a comparable place in the book of Amos there is a similar narrative of the prophet presenting himself at a shrine (probably on a day of festival) and not finding himself welcome.

9:1-9 Hosea continues his attack on the cult. In the previous chapters the targets had been idols, altars, and sacrifices; in the present chapter he chooses the most culpable example of cultic apostasy: a harvest festival. Most likely this was the autumn festival of Tabernacles or Booths, also known as the "feast of the LORD" (v. 5; Judg. 21:19-21; Deut. 16:13-15; Lev. 23:39-43). The surroundings, with their constant reminders of the Baals and of the fertility ideology, inevitably produced, as we have noted, some of the themes and thinking of the earliest chapters in Hosea. The subject of harvest also prompts one to ask what, if any, is the place now of the wind/whirlwind theme (Hos. 8:7). Do we find the principles of unwelcome harvest and disproportionate response present in ch. 9, or do we find any other reminders of that proverbial verse? I think we do. Israel's turning to the Canaanite cult in order to secure fertility of flock, field, and womb is constantly frustrated by God; but he does not stop there. He never leaves his people to their own devices; they are not allowed to go their own way. There is always the whirlwind harvest to be reaped. The people have corrupted Yahweh's festivals; they shall go where none can be held. They have made the land unclean; they shall be driven from the land after it had been made a wilderness. They want to go to Egypt for refuge; they shall find there derision and death. They mock a prophet; they shall be captured and hated. The wind/whirlwind principles are there in plenty, but how they function is hard to say. Is the prophet consciously exemplifying a process to which he has given paradigmatic and classical expression in 8:7, or is it—and perhaps this is more probable—that some of the ways of God with his wayward people found in this verse are a memorable articulation for all time that cannot be improved upon? To be chosen means that at times one's sown winds are reaped as whirlwinds.

Was Hosea, as a prophet, asked to speak, or did he thrust himself forward to thunder that the whole festive proceeding should cease? The combination of "rejoice" and "exult" is not common. It occurs for the first time in Hosea, and "exult" is not found in either the Pentateuch or the Former Prophets. We conclude that the words so used indicate the kind of commotion that belonged to the pagan, idolatrous happenings that Hosea was witnessing. It was exulting "like the peoples," and we have to imagine that this included the frenzy and licentious screaming that one expected from the Gentiles but not from Israel. After the command to stop comes the reason for the protest. Surrounded perhaps by very obvious sexual indulgence and by the worship of either the Baals or of Yahweh being treated like a Baal, Hosea castigates Israel's harlotry—of making love for gain. The gain was either financial or— far more likely—the gain was the grain, the flax, the wine, and the oil which they took to be their fee for unlawful sex and unlawful sacrifice.

After the reason for his outburst in the second half of 9:1 Hosea gives God's initial response—the "unwelcome harvest" response (vv. 1, 2). That is, God frustrates the central purpose of the corrupt rituals by not allowing them to produce the results they were designed for. The law of cause and effect as Israel had come to understand it was broken. All they did in shrines and on the threshing floor was with the single aim of aiding fertility and ensuring there would be food and drink for the coming year. Hosea announces that this is not so. "Threshing floor and wine vat shall not feed them, and the new wine shall fail them." It would be surprising if this were not greeted by laughter mixed with resentment and contempt. Wasn't this a harvest festival? All was safely gathered in, and most of the festivities were already made more festive by generous drafts of the new wine. If as is reported in v. 7, the assembly finally dismissed the prophet as a fool and mad, it would be strange if this judgment were not preceded by some preliminary skirmishes. Hosea's retort was ready and was more than adequate; it went beyond the "unwelcome harvest" to the disproportionate reaction principle. The harvest may indeed be in, but it would not nourish Israel because Israel would not be there to enjoy it. Ephraim was finished as Ephraim; they were going to Egypt and to slavery or to Assyria where there was only inedible food (cf. Amos 7:17).

The expression "the land of the LORD" (the land of Yahweh) occurs here for the first time in the OT. No doubt it means much and implies more. It is Yahweh's land and no-one else's. Especially it is not the Baals' land as many in Israel seemed to think. It is Yahweh's and is at his disposal. He is the landlord, and he has chosen the land for his people and his people for this land. The "marriage" of Israel to the land was parallel to the marriage between God and Israel, or perhaps the former was an extension of the latter. This land was not just acreage of food-producing earth; there was plenty of that in the rest of the world, all of which was Yahweh's (Exod. 19:5). This land was uniquely God's in his relation to Israel. It was symbolic, sacramental land, part of the total "package" of God's saving work with Israel and through Israel. The saving history had never been separate from the law. In that first foreshadowing of what was to come, in the time of the patriarchs, the land was promised to Abraham and his successors. At the time of the Exodus his saving work included the gift of the Promised Land (Deut. 26:9), and Israel's faithfulness and possession of the land were always in principle intimately tied together (Deut. 28:63ff.; 30:15ff.). In the wilderness the land was the hoped-for goal; in the time of Joshua

the land was both gracious gift and proof of God's power and faithfulness. But this all changed after the settlement, and the land and
its ways and traditions became the great temptation. Before it is
enjoyed, before it is possessed, the land is a source of faith; yet once
it is theirs it becomes a stumbling block and a cause of revolt. In
Hos. 9:3 these theological overtones are present, if not paramount.
In being driven off Yahweh's land and condemned to life in Egypt
and Assyria they would naturally not be able to enjoy the fruits of
Canaan, and this we have stressed above. But there is more being
said than this. The break with Canaan is not just emigration or
another wilderness wandering; the break with the land is a break
with the LORD of the land. What began with Abraham and
climaxed with Moses is now finished. Ephraim (Israel) in an "unclean" land is a corpse.

   Hosea's references to the cult are usually wholly critical and unsympathetic because he is addressing worship in its debased form.
Verses 4 and 5 are equally negative, but negative in a different way
because they assume a very positive place for the kind of worship
which is not debased. Hosea is no longer speaking of pagan distor-
tions in Canaan but of the absence of true worship when God's
people are already out of Yahweh's land and in exile. There appear
to be two assumptions underlying the verses. One is that which is
present in most of the Pentateuch, namely that preservation of the
covenant relationship is dependent upon ritual which is performed
according to the law. In Exodus, once the covenant is ratified in ch.
24, the next step is to plan and construct the tabernacle which will
house the covenant cult. Then in the next book, Leviticus, we are
given the details of how to conduct the cultic rituals in the tabernacle. To live in Yahweh's land involves proper worship of Yahweh
in his land. The second assumption underlying these verses is that
once one is out of Yahweh's land and exiled in a place such as Assyria or Egypt it is no longer possible to satisfy the legal demands
for valid worship. This accords with Deut. 12; 26:14, etc., and
parallels the view of the psalmists in Pss. 42, 43 and 137. Hosea
doesn't ask "How shall we sing the LORD'S song in a foreign land?"
He just knows it is impossible. It cannot be done. Hosea 9:4 has
no questions, only statements of what is essential but impossible
outside Yahweh's land. The people will not be able to pour liba-
tions or offer acceptable sacrifices. The bread cannot be used in
worship because it has all become like "mourners' bread," that is,

unclean, and will defile and not purify. It cannot even be taken into the place where worship might be proposed "for their bread shall be for their hunger only" or "their bread serves their gullet."

Isn't bread for hunger? Is it not to serve the gullet? Of course. The significant word here is "only," and in this context it is very significant. The cult which should have lifted people's hearts to God had been treated as a source of sensual pleasure and as a technique for getting the fruits of the earth. The sacrifices given to heal a broken relationship with God had been turned into occasions of feasting and gluttony. Now bread is added to the list. It is regarded as nothing more than bodily food. These denials of the spiritual side of life had been Israel's doing in the first place; but God takes the people at their word and puts them in a situation where altar and sacrifice become impossible and bread is merely bread that satisfies the body. The implications of the limited bread parallel the sending into exile and the termination of the saving history. Life with God is ending. Flesh is only for feasting and not for forgiveness. Bread may keep the body alive but has lost all power to mediate God's life to mankind. Israel is to be locked into a materialistic universe. The sacramental principle is a thing of the past. The ladder set up between heaven and earth which Jacob dreamed of was merely a dream. Access to God—the heart of the religious quest anywhere—was now denied to Israel.

The statements of v. 4 are followed by the question of v. 5. What, in a foreign land, would they do when the time for Tabernacles came round again? In form it is a question, but a rhetorical one and therefore in reality a statement. The Feast of Tabernacles was ended. For the north the feast had been started by Jeroboam, who had established it to prevent his people from going south to Jerusalem (1 Kgs. 12:32-33; 8:2). The feast had become an essential part of the nation's life, and life as Yahweh's people was now unthinkable without it. Hosea's message was that no matter what they thought about it, they had not been celebrating the feast for ages, for a debased ritual is worse than no ritual. Therefore it was finished. Better unclean bread abroad and no festival than a people deluded into thinking that the Holy One of Israel could be honored or even pacified by the then current blasphemy.

In Hos. 9:6 it is better to read "from destruction" (RSV margin) than "Assyria." The meaning then is "For behold, they flee from destruction—Egypt shall gather them, Memphis shall bury them." Points already made are being hammered home. Hosea surveys the crowd which had gathered for the festival. He has already taunted them with his rhetorical question about future festival days. Now we imagine him saying "Will you be gathered then, as you are gathered today"? He answers the question himself. "Yes, you will be gathered, but not for festival. Egypt will gather you for a funeral, and Memphis (site of many tombs and place of mortuary expertise) will bury you. And as for your precious land where you are gathered today, it will be cared for—by nettles and thorns. The jungle will take over."

Was this threat met by laughter? If it was, his hearers could not be blamed too much. The contrast between the fun and games of harvest home and the dismal picture Hosea was painting has humorous possibilities, if we don't have too much respect for the prophet and haven't understood the power of the prophetic word to create what it announces. If there was derision, it in turn was confronted by a program for the funeral (v. 7). Verse 5 had spoken of "the day of appointed festival." That was a date everyone knew. "The day of the feast of the LORD" needed no programs; the people needed no reminders. The days of punishment and recompense were different. These were not annual events by any means, and the days and times were only known to those to whom they had been revealed. But certainly the times were fixed, and Israel's ignorance of them could not alter the fact that they were fixed. Soon the power would be expelled. Israel may scoff today, but in due time "Israel shall know it."

The second part of the verse ("The prophet is a fool, the man of the spirit is mad") is perhaps the only place in the book where we learn how Hosea's message was received by his contemporaries. It is comparable in some ways to the exchange between Amos and the priest in Amos 7:10ff., but without the specific details which the Amos passage provides. Was this contemptuous assessment of Hosea general, or was this spoken by representatives of the cultic prophets who were a combination of "the voice of the people" and propagandists for those in authority? Either way, we can take it as the majority opinion that the prophet was looked upon as both mentally deficient and emotionally disturbed. Such a valuation was almost inevitable. Hosea saw life through God's eyes; his critics judged with their senses and by the values of their made-to-measure gods. It was the "Corinthian" situation eight hundred years before Paul's day (1 Cor. 1), where one person's wisdom is another's insanity and vice versa. Another reason why such a reaction was to be expected is that it is the best manner of dealing with unwanted criticism. If someone is criticizing you and your conscience is beginning to tell you that there may be something in the criticism, and you realize that if you admit the criticism you will have to change, then the best and speediest defense is to convince yourself that your critic is crazy and that what he says is rubbish and nonsense. A true prophet must be a fool and madman to the world, and the world's only hope is when the prophet's folly is recognized as the true wisdom. Hosea's folly had to wait a long time before it was seen to be the truth. Most likely he died still a "fool" and a "madman." His immediate response was both proof of his sanity and an example of his great wisdom—a combination of psychological and theological insight. His explanation of the people's hatred towards him was that it arose from their own sense of guilt. If this is true, we have to recognize that at least they were not shameless; their consciences were not dead, merely powerless to will repentance. They were disturbed in spirit, and so the unconscious solution for them came in turning self-hatred into hatred of the one who had disturbed them. Their hatred and bitterness, in a roundabout way, was also evidence that Hosea was right and that his arrows of criticism were right on target.

Do Hos. 9:8 and 9 also belong to Hosea's response to the people's venom? There is good reason to believe they do. We shall take them as spoken by Hosea on the day of the festival without prejudice to the question as to whether vv. 10ff. come from the same occasion or not. Verse 8 is one of the most problematic in the whole book. How do we relate "my God" and "his God"? Who is the watchman, Ephraim or the prophet? Is the fowler's snare set to trap the prophet, or is the prophet a snare to the people? And who is the prophet anyway? The translators of the RSV have had to make their own decisions on these and other questions. I shall follow their translation, except that I would wish to leave open the possibility that the prophet may be both trap and the one trapped.

The close link between verses 7 and 8 is clear. Apart from other considerations they both include the word "prophet," and even more significantly they both contain a rare word translated in both verses as "hostility" or (with RSV) "hatred." Plainly these verses belong together; therefore, as we have understood "prophet" to

refer to Hosea himself in v. 7, we shall assume that it does so in
v. 8. We shall also assume that it is the prophet speaking in both
verses 8 and 9. The watchman image has appeared already in 5:8
and 8:1; now the word is openly applied to Hosea himself. Later
prophets (Jer. 6:17; Ezek. 3:17; Isa. 56:10) have the term applied
to them, but Hosea was the first to use it as far as we know. Hosea
5:8 and 8:1 have already given us some idea of how Hosea understood the responsibilities of a watchman. Here in ch. 9 he further
qualifies the term when applied to the prophet. First, the RSV
would be more correct if it translated v. 8a,b "The prophet is the
watchman of Ephraim with my God" (i.e., reading the consonan-
tal Hebrew text as *'im* and not *'am*). This makes clear not only that
Hosea is watching Ephraim but that he is doing it for and in association with God. Perhaps the use of the pronoun "my" both
aligns the prophet closely with God and separates Ephraim from
him. God is the prophet's God in a way that "he is not Ephraim's."
Thus God and Hosea together are watching Ephraim. What is
their purpose? Normally the task of a watchman is to protect. He
watches for the enemy and sounds the alarm when he approaches.
The context compels us to accept a less simple understanding here,
especially if we allow for the possibility that the fowler's snare was
set not so much for the prophet as for Ephraim. This watchman
has a wider brief than most, and a good deal of ambivalence and
flexibility must be allowed for. At least two things determine the
meaning of the prophet as watchman in this passage: first, the immediate context of the festival, and second, the fact that he was
watchman with his God.

The people had called the prophet a fool and said that he was
mad. Hosea retorts that he is a watchman who is neither foolish
nor mad. He is the opposite of what they think. Fools are dull and
unreasonable; watchmen are supremely alert and reasonable. Madness is a threat to society; watchmen are guarantors of its security.
The main understanding of Hosea's function as watchman must,
however, come from the fact that he is "the watchman of Ephraim
with my God." The watching is a joint effort but the job description, needless to say, comes from God's work. This is what the
whole book is about: the work of death and life, destruction and
construction, lament and praise. It is a work of paradox and of
supreme reason. Hosea serves and watches within God's norms
and values. He is the eyes and lips of the law, called to foolishness

and hostility, to be a snare and inevitably to be snared. The uncertainty in the second half of the verse is confusing but quite appropriate. Given the conditions of Hosea's employment as watchman, it is to be expected that he would both threaten and be threatened, be hostile and experience hostility.

9:9   This verse, which may be the last part of the festival narrative, centers on an historical reference, the first of four in ch. 9. Hosea's revilers are accused of corrupting themselves (or acting basely) as in "the days of Gibeah." This is followed by a concluding promise of judgment which is almost identical with 8:13b. Hosea's practice of quoting historical events is a feature of his style and begins as early as 1:4. Reference to "the days of Gibeah" occurs also in 10:9, and it seems reasonable to assume that the two references are to the same days and not to two distinct events or sets of events that occurred in Gibeah. Opinion divides between two possible answers to the question "Which days?" King Saul lived at Gibeah in the land of Benjamin (1 Sam. 10:26; 11:4), and it was with Saul that the monarchy began. Do "the days of Gibeah" therefore symbolize the monarchy because it was in Gibeah that the monarchy began and therefore Gibeah could be regarded as the cradle of an institution which produced so much corruption? This is less possible than the second suggestion, which is that the expression recalls the horrifyingly shameless episode narrated in Judg. 19–21. The correspondence with Hosea's times is close. In both periods individuals are treated abominably; uncontrolled lust is at the source; God himself is responsible for the punishment, and terrible destruction falls upon Israel. In Judg. 20:34 we read "but the Benjaminites did not know that disaster was close upon them," and then in v. 36 "so the Benjaminites saw that they were defeated." Perhaps Hosea saw a word for his own day in these traditions.

9:10-17   The historical reference in Hos. 9:9 is followed by a section which includes two other major historical recollections: Baal-peor (v. 10) and Gilgal (v. 15). Although the wilderness is also mentioned (v. 10), the recollections of Baal-peor and Gilgal are more significant; indeed, it is around these two that the whole section revolves. Thus the section divides into two parts: vv. 10-14, which develop out of the Baal-peor episode, and vv. 15-17, which have Gilgal as their focal point. These similarities are not the only ones which exist between the two parts; there are parallels both in form and in content. Each part has its source in a place where momentous events occurred in the past and which has acquired a certain symbolic and representational value. Mention is made of the sins associated with the place and the continuing comparable sins in the present. Threats and judgment follow which in both cases include lack of fertility, population depletion, and the death of children at God's hand. Finally, each part concludes a divine speech with a prophetic utterance (vv. 14 and 17); that in v. 14 is clearly a prayer for disaster to fall, and that in v. 17 can be read as a prayer which is in effect a curse. Continuities with what has gone before are everywhere; two deserve special mention. We have met the emphasis on cultic and kingly sins before, especially in chs. 7 and 8. The two parts of this section divide along these lines: 9:10-14 concentrates on the cultic ways, while vv. 15-17 are more concerned with the sins of the leaders. The second continuity is with 8:7. In both parts of the present section it is not difficult to see both the unwelcome harvest theme and the disproportionate effect.

9:10-14   The prophet who gave us the phrase "like people, like priest" (4:9) might also have given us the expression "like past, like present." Frequently, and especially in the latter part of the book, the principle is demonstrated. What Israel was, it still is. What Israel is, it has been from the earliest days. But this only applies to a continuity of sin. In the very rare instances where Israel was commendable in the past the principle breaks down. Moments that were praiseworthy were unique. One such moment is referred to in 9:10, where a very rare election tradition is quoted (cf. Jer. 2:2). According to this, Israel was chosen in the wilderness because they were precious and desirable. Israel was like the unexpected grape in the desert, like the early, costly, out-of-season fig. The "fathers" were chosen not only because of God's gracious love but because they were choice. Hosea sees nothing similar to these favorable qualities in the present. The wilderness election had nothing to bequeath to the Israel of Hosea's time. Contemporary Israel was a direct descendent and exact likeness of the time of Baal-peor, where they first encountered Baal and immediately were seduced into consecrating themselves to him.

This incident of apostasy is recorded in Num. 25:1-5. Peor was a mountain (Num. 23:28) where a Baal was worshipped. A city named Beth-peor (Deut. 3:29; 4:46) had grown up there, presumably around the shrine. There Israel first "played the harlot" and, so Hosea implies, never stopped doing so. Baal-peor set the direction for the rest of Israel's history and overlaid completely the influence of God's teaching through his law. Israel's identity as a kingdom of priests and a holy nation was short-lived. That identity existed only until they reached Beth-peor, where it was changed completely. The process of change is indicated with the same insight that was shown in the final part of Hos. 9:7. Israel consecrates itself to Baal (or "Shame") with all the devotion that a Nazirite possesses when he is consecrated to Yahweh. The result is that Israel becomes "detestable" or "an abhorrent thing." The Hebrew word here is one that is often used to describe idols; so what Hosea is saying is that by worshipping idols they become like idols themselves, and the shift occurs because of misplaced love. You become what you love, or what you worship, says the prophet. You are a reflection of your "sacred." That to which you give priority and which you make your absolute, that which establishes your norms and values, that which tells you what is good and true and beautiful is what determines your identity and tells you who you are. But what if the thing you worship is a "nothing," a creation of your own imagination or lusts, like the Baals for instance? This, strange as it may seem, is of no significance. Even though "the thing they loved" is of their own manufacture, its potency to seduce or to change their identity is not limited. The whole of Scripture affirms with Hosea the strange paradox that idols are "nothings," creatures of illusion; and yet at the same time they are the greatest evil because they threaten the whole of life—in this world and the next.

Hosea's assumption is that Israel turned to the Baals because they were experts in the area of fertility—presumably to make up for Yahweh's imagined deficiency in an agricultural realm. Verse 11, returning to themes first propounded in ch. 2, speaks of the punishment which will fall. As usual the punishment is made to fit the crime—and more. Ephraim (or "Ephraim's glory") is likened to a flock of birds which flies away. The "glory" is obviously in contrast with the "shame" in 9:10. I prefer therefore to take "glory" as indicating Yahweh himself. Yahweh leaves, and what is the result? Granted the current beliefs about the power of the Baals, the one area Ephraim would expect not to be affected was that of birth, pregnancy, and conception. These were the Baals' responsibility, not Yahweh's, so his absence surely would make no difference to them. The reality is the reverse. Fertility is Yahweh's domain (like everything else); when Yahweh leaves, fertility ceases. This is the unwelcome, totally unexpected harvest of punishment. But there is more to come. There is now the disproportionate reaction in v. 12. Even if children are born, they will not be reared because God will bereave them. The salvation history included, in its beginnings, the death of the firstborn of the Egyptians. But this history had been short-lived; in reality it had only lasted until Baal-peor. Since then God's people had been apostate. Now they were to experience the great reversal in a fearsome form. It had been terrible for Egypt to lose its firstborn. For Israel it would be far worse; all their children would die, and none would be born. The woe is on God's own people, for they would suffer the worst possible disaster: the departure of God himself. With God's departure would come the end of their history, the end of fertility, and the end of life itself because he is the living God, the giver of life.

The original form of 13a is unclear, and its interpretation depends in part on how it is to be related to the second part of the verse. I take the verse as throwing the blame for the coming disaster squarely on Ephraim's shoulders. God's departure is the immediate cause of this coming chaos, but Ephraim is responsible for having driven him away by their behavior. As already pointed out, vv. 10-14 are mainly concerned with Israel's spiritual harlotry which commenced with the Baal-peor episode; but spiritual and political harlotry are twins—Siamese twins, and where there is one there is the other. Verse 13 appears to refer to the reliance on Assyria and Egypt. This political apostasy has had the opposite effect from what was intended. The motive had been protection and safety; the end result was to lead their offspring on to the spears of the hunter. The inevitable slaughter was the work of Ephraim's own hands.

The words of God now yield place to a prophetic prayer, and, as so often, we are conscious of similarities with Amos. In visions and auditions Amos learned of horrors that were to befall Israel (Amos 7:1, 4). Responding, as a prophet was expected to, he prayed for "Jacob" that they might be forgiven (Amos 7:2, 5). The prayer was heard. God "repented" and the threatened terrors were withdrawn. A third vision (Amos 7:7-9) includes within it the words "I will never again pass by them." Amos understands this as a warning that the time for intercession is over, so in this and the succeeding visionary accounts there is no prayer (Amos 8:1-3; 9:1-4), only acceptance. In Hos. 9:14 Hosea is in a quandary. He wishes to pray for his people, but how is he to pray? He begins instinctively "Give them, O LORD . . . ," but then stops. God has already said in numerous ways what he is about to give his people. Was Hosea to choose the least menacing punishment from the list he had already compiled and ask God to forget the rest?

In his confused compassion the prophet asks a question: "What wilt thou give"? Hosea's answer to the question should perhaps be heard, in part as a continuation of his confused compassion and in part as the result of a difficult choice. God has threatened infertility, so in his prayer for "miscarrying womb and dry breasts" Hosea is not opposing all that God intends; indeed, infertility is perhaps the least of that catalogue of evils which included the end of history, the end of life, and the departure of God. It would be better if God were to be content with this one punishment and forego the rest. But if the rest did come, it would be better for those without children to be slaughtered, without pregnant wives whose wombs might be torn open. Is the prayer then both modified curse and partial blessing?

In Amos there is a conciseness and clarity which is not so obvious in Hosea. These prayers are a case in point. Amos is sharp and clear-cut. He prays and the prayer is answered; when the time for intercession is ended he does not pray. Hosea hesitates and questions. Like the God he speaks of, he reveals an internal dialogue, as tenderness and severity battle inside him. Was Hosea a self-questioning man who saw all sides to an issue and then made God partly in his own image? I prefer to stand the question on its head and make it a statement. Hosea was led a little further than Amos into God's inner sanctuary and was permitted to hear God's dialogue with himself. As living proof of his conviction that we become like the thing we love, Hosea's inner conversations reflect those of the God he loved and worshipped. The dialogue in Hosea mirrors the dialogue in God.

9:15-17   The pattern we have investigated in vv. 10-14 is now repeated, but this time the order of political and cultic unfaithful-

ness is reversed. In vv. 10-14 cultic error beginning at Beth-peor is
at the center, with hints of political apostasy in v. 13. In vv. 15-17
we take the references to "princes" in v. 15 as confirming that the
order is reversed. But much depends on how we interpret what
"Gilgal" is meant to imply in v. 15. Other occurrences of the name
in Hosea are clearly part of the prophet's protest against the cult
(4:15; 12:11). This is supported by Amos 4:4; 5:5, but the last
words of Hos. 9:15 ("all their princes are rebels" or "all their
leaders are misleaders") give reason for further consideration and
prompt the search for alternative meanings attached to Gilgal. The
search leads to the conclusion that "Gilgal" here is meant to point
us in the direction of the monarchy, for it was at Gilgal that the first
king, Saul, was inaugurated (1 Sam. 11:14). While I do not agree
with commentators who insist that for Hosea kingship in itself was
evil, it is perfectly clear that the prophet saw the monarchy in Israel as corrupt and a source of great evil. We see in Gilgal, then, the
sign of corrupt kingship and of all in Israel's life that denied the
kingship of God over his people.

At Gilgal God began to "hate" his people, or "became their
enemy." Had he not hated them at Beth-peor? Is this a further stage
in a deteriorating relationship? Such questions are out of place.
Hosea is prophet and poet, not historian or logician. The order indicated is theological, not chronological. Political harlotry flows
from religious unfaithfulness and idolatry. Israel's first errors with
regard to kingship were in their unwillingness to trust wholly in
Yahweh as king. The Baal-peor sin is the prior one; the wrongs that
began at Gilgal, the political wrongs, are derivative—derivative but
desperately serious. The kingly crimes mean that the rightful king
will banish his subjects from his house (or land) and the king who
had loved them would love them no more. To love a traitor or
mutineer is another form of treachery or mutiny. The chronological question appears again. Did the love cease when the hate began,
or did love and hate coexist until the 8th century? Undoubtedly the
latter. God was the loving enemy, and a love-hate relationship had
existed from the first murmurings against God. That love now
ends, says Hosea, not because God has ceased to love but because
his love has been rejected. Love, the final victor, has times of failure
when faced with obduracy. Hosea 9:16 repeats in new words the
message of vv. 11-13, with the help of a pun on "Ephraim" and

"fruit," which in Hebrew have the same consonants. The Hebrew reads "The fruitful shall be fruitless." God's punishment will be the end to fertility, and God himself will become the slayer of any surviving children.

It is possible to translate the first line of v. 17 as a prayer or request. The parallel with vv. 10-14 which ends in prayer inclines us to read "Let my God reject them." After two intercessions Amos realized that the end really must come (Amos 7:8b; 8:2). Hosea seems to have come to the same conclusion. In this "prayer" there is neither hesitation nor dialogue. God is adamant, and the prophetic word of rejection goes forth with its power to implement its own message. The confidence and precision rest on two things. First, Hosea is able to say "my God" because he is certain that he has stood in the council of God and heard God's decree that Israel will be cast off. God is his God—not in a possessive way, and not only in contrast with Ephraim, who has been rejected. The prophet can say "my God" because at this awesome moment he is abiding in God and God in him. The word he utters is the word of the One whom he can call "my God." Second, Hosea speaks without hesitation of rejection "because they have not hearkened to him." Israel's election was not wholly unconditional, and the first and greatest condition was obedience. This was lacking, and thus rejection was inevitable. Obedience was the means of reception, like hands that accept a gift. If the hands are not there, the gift cannot be taken. God's rejection was predetermined by Israel's nonreception. It was reaction more than action.

Rejected by God, then, what does the future hold for Ephraim? "They shall be wanderers among the nations." At the Exodus the power of fate had been broken. Chosen to be God's peculiar people, they were free of the gods of the nations and of the kings of the nations. They were also liberated from the powers of nature and from the fates, because God is supreme, above all earthly and heavenly powers. In their rejection by God the people were now subject to the "principalities and powers" and were fated to be wanderers. Jacob had wandered to Egypt in search of food, but Hosea sees not merely a return to a patriarchal life of wandering. He sees a reversion to the state of Cain, who was a fugitive and wanderer with everyone's hand against him. Israel had chosen a life with the nations as any other nation, but this was not possible.

Only two possibilities faced them: either to be the bride of Yahweh or to be a wanderer among the nations, aliens without a real identity. God had created Israel for himself. In him was their only rest; without him there was only restlessness.

CHAPTER TEN
Hosea 10:1-15

THORN AND THISTLE (10:1-8)

There is considerable agreement that these verses form a unit and that therefore they should be exegeted in close relationship with one another. Reasons for such a decision are: 1) The first and last verses include the word "Israel." This is one of Hosea's devices for marking beginnings and endings of subsections. 2) The address throughout is similar. It is not God speaking but someone speaking about God — presumably the prophet. 3) The eight verses divide into four strophes of two verses each. The first three strophes, vv. 1-2, 3-4, 5-6, have the same form—several lines of accusation culminating in a threat. 4) Each of the first three strophes is devoted to one of Hosea's three great topics: cult, king, and calf, in that order. The fourth strophe seems to conclude the section by including all three.

If the prophet is the one speaking here, to whom then is he speaking? What is the likely setting of the unit? It seems he is speaking to an audience *about* Israel and about Israel's relationship with God; the audience is not included in the accusation. This is third-person speech and not second-person. The unit reflects neither confrontation with the people as in 9:7-8 nor prayer to God as in 9:14. A possible audience is some group sympathetic to Hosea's point of view, with whom he could share the revelations he had received and jointly reflect upon them. Such a fellowship could consist of prophets, Levites, or his own disciples who preserved and transmitted his words (cf. Isa. 8:16). It is therefore not inconceivable that his listeners were in some way co-creators of the prophesies as we have them.

Were the words of the dialoguing God not only conveyed through the medium of the dialoguing prophet, but were they conveyed only after further dialogue and reflection within an inner circle of supporters? Even Jesus Christ needed the support of his disciples and had long conversations with them. How much more would a prophet need a creative, supportive "plausibility structure." No man is an island, not even a prophet. Furthermore, this group might not only have had a creative place in Hosea's delivering the oracles; they may well have been the ones who presented and edited the oracles of their leaders and companions. Thus the creative companions might well have contributed both before and after Hosea's own preaching.

Even though the form, address, and audience of this section are novel, there is much that follows on from what has gone before. The cult, king, and calf subjects are not new; neither are the accusations, threats, and promises of judgment. The historical references, although more prominent in Hos. 10:9ff., are not absent in vv. 1-8. Samaria, Assyria, and Beth-aven (or Bethel) all receive dishonorable mention, while in v. 1 the "luxuriant vine" links onto the "grapes in the wilderness" of 9:10.

10:1-2 The "luxuriant vine" shares another similarity with "grapes in the wilderness." Not only is the vine/grapes image common to both; they also both start off longer passages by saying something positive about Israel. This makes them a rather rare usage in Hosea's prophecy. The approving note is not all it appears to be, as we shall see; but first let us note how the positive beginning enhances the profound sense of tragedy that pervades 10:1-8. The verses begin with luxuriance and prosperity; they end with such unnamable horrors impending that the mountains crushing them would be preferable. The same theme is in all parts: all good things—fruitfulness, improvement, cult, kings, priests—turn sour and cause evil and disaster. Crimes are listed, but what exactly makes them into the kind of crimes that deserve the looming judgments outlined is not immediately obvious. Thus one inevitably asks why good always becomes bad, and light becomes dark. Where is the worm in the rose? The answer is found in v. 2: "Their heart is false," or "Their heart is divided." Here is the dual heart, or dual will; it is being two-faced that poisons everything. Do the people serve God and mammon, or do their altars face both Yahweh and Baal? This we are not told; but within each verse we are warned to look for the false heart.

Israel had been plagued with prosperity. Canaan really was a
land flowing with milk and honey, despite its stony appearance. Of
course we know, and God and Hosea knew, that the fruitfulness
came from God. But Israel turned to the Baals in thanksgiving, and
no doubt with not a little self-congratulation at their own smart-
ness. They had contextualized very successfully. They had borrowed the local religious techniques with little difficulty. They were
flexible, liberal, open, forward-looking, and progressive. They
were not afraid of innovation and, what's more, the new techniques worked. They were prosperous, rich, and well fed.
Moreover they were grateful and prudent. If the altars worked,
then they would have more of them and see that they were never
short of sacrifices. It was good business sense to reinvest more and
more of the profits in the system that earned them. The altars multiplied, and the forbidden pillars (Deut. 12:3) grew bigger and better. Israel applied the standard of "success" and decided everything
was sound. And so it was—except the theology. Prosperity, altars,
thanksgiving, petition — all are good if the altars are places of
petitioning Yahweh and thanking him for the prosperity.

10:3-4   It is impossible to be dogmatic about either the translation or the interpretation of these two verses. Who is the king in
Hos. 10:3—Yahweh, or the Baals whose altars and pillars are to be
destroyed, or the present monarch? How much here is quotation,
and how much is Hosea's own comment to his companions? These
are but a few of the puzzles. The following proposals have kept
guesswork to a minimum, but nothing more can be claimed. I assume the "now" of v. 3 links onto the "now" of v. 2b. This in effect
turns the "now" of v. 3 into "then" because the utterance of Israel,
"We have no king. . . ," is actually what the prophet imagines they
will say when the disaster has struck. We conjecture that Hosea has
spoken vv. 1 and 2 to his listeners. He then hears a future confession of the people which admits that they have lost both king and
God. There the "quotation" ends, and the rest of v. 3 and v. 4 is
Hosea's own comment. The Jerusalem Bible translates as follows:

Then they will say,
"We have no king,
because we have not feared Yahweh."
But what can a king do for us?

> Words, words! False oaths! Alliances!
> And judgment is only a poisonous weed that thrives
> in the furrows of the field.

It would be surprising if the imagined "quotation" were not related in some way to Israel's experience of kingship in Hosea's own time, and there has been no shortage of suggestions as to what the concrete context was. The total absence of any real clue in the text surely implies that the transmitters of the text did not think the context too important. If it had been important, then they were very remiss in failing to provide some guidance. We therefore must hear these questions and statements in a general manner rather than as comment on a specific occasion. As such we find in the verses confirmation of what Hosea (and most of the OT) says elsewhere about kings—that is, that kings and Yahweh belong together. If the king is Yahweh's appointee and endowed with his spirit, then all is well and *shalom* reigns. If the people do not fear the LORD and set up their own leaders, then no matter what they call them they are not kings; they are disasters, menaces, and evildoers. Contemptuously the prophet gives his opinion on these pseudo-kings, and he does it by running through a list of what a king is supposed to do. Kings have to talk, of course; but these kings only talk. They're all talk and no action; their words are removed from reality. Kings have to make oaths, particularly at their coronation, and these oaths should bind them to be good shepherds of their people. Not so these kings; they are more like wolves. Kings have to make a covenant with God and with the people, agreeing to protect them and rule wisely. These kings break such covenants with impunity and make fateful alliances with idols and the nations. Above all, kings stand for justice in society, justice that should ensure peace, security, and prosperity. Our kings, says Hosea, stand for the opposite: not grain but weeds, not food but poison (Amos 5:7; 6:12).

10:5-6   The false heart had made good altars bad, and a gift of kingship into poison. The same falsity had chosen a man-made idol of an animal in preference to the God who had saved them. The altars were destroyed, the pseudo-kings exposed, and now we see the end of the "calf of Beth-aven" (Hos. 10:5 comments on 8:5-6). How is it that an idol finds itself alongside altars and kings? Altars and kings are not in themselves evil; it is only in a distorted and corrupt form that they become instruments of sin. The same cannot be said of idols, which have no positive role in Israel's life, only negative. We cannot contemplate an undistorted or uncorrupted idol; they are a source of distortion and corruption. It is true that idols in general have no place in the present series, but the calf is different. For some decades there has been general agreement among OT scholars that the calf was not an idol to begin with but a pedestal or seat for Yahweh. It did not begin in opposition to Yahweh but quite literally as his support. What started off as something apparently innocuous ended up quite differently, as these verses make plain. Perhaps this reinforced Israel's vehement prohibition of all graven images, whatever their purpose and function. If something intended to raise Yahweh, almost to be his throne, could ultimately dethrone him, then all visible representations were dangerous and to be avoided. Maybe the sin was in thinking God needed support (2 Sam. 6ff.), other than the cherubim in Jerusalem which were his throne. Therefore, what began as a kindly, honoring intention had in it sufficient unbelief to produce an odious substitute for Yahweh that stole away all but a few hearts. In these possibilities there has been food for thought for later generations of both Jews and Christians.

Hosea 10:5 pictures a people wholly led astray by a false faith. The threatened calf meant a threatened people. Instead of being joined to Yahweh and knowing security, they had joined their hearts to a calf and were trembling, not only for themselves but for the calf. That which they relied upon was unreliable. The vocabulary of the next phrases tells the story of the Canaanization of the cult. For the first time in the OT priests are described as "idolatrous," a word normally reserved for functionaries in an alien/pagan religion. The verbs "mourn" and "wail" carry with them overtones of the ecstatic unrestrained worship of the Baals. But this is hardly worship; it is more a wake, a dirge over the demise of their God. The golden trappings and priceless regalia had gone, perhaps contributing to some of the tribute paid to the king of Assyria. The calf's glory had already departed. Now it was the turn of the calf: "The thing itself shall be carried to Assyria, as tribute to the great king" (v. 6). All ends in shame — shame for Ephraim, shame for Israel—because of the shamed idol. The irony is intense and is a worthy precursor to two Isaianic treatments of idolatry (Isa. 41:5ff.; 44:9ff.). The protector of Israel cannot protect itself; the symbol of strength is led captive; the mark of fertility and new life is lifeless. The words go far beyond any irony inherent in Israel's folly; they reach to the darkest tragedy of human existence. Adam at home with God in paradise exchanged that condition for exile because an animal mocked and an apple beckoned. Israel was essential humanity in repudiating the God of love for the calf of shame.

10:7-8   The fourth strophe can best be understood as a partial summary of Hos. 10:1-6 and as a conclusion which carries a strong air of finality about it. It must be confessed that the notion that here we have a rounding-off of the section does contribute a little to the interpretation, but this is preferable to the guesswork which might be the alternative.

"Samaria's king" (literally, 'Samaria, her king') is unusual. Strictly speaking there was no king of Samaria. The phrase could continue the theme of vv. 5-6 and indicate the calf of Samaria, which could be thought of as perishing "like a ship on the face of the waters." I prefer however to take the word "king" literally and see the verse as prophesying the fall of Samaria and the end of the monarchy. This still allows direct continuity with v. 6 because this would be an important part of the promised shame. If the calf is not present in v. 7, it is included in v. 8 among "the high places of Aven, the sin of Israel." The summary has ended where v. 1 began —with the altars; and their destruction is once more a demonstration of poetic justice. The altars had been there to fuel the fertility process. This they will continue to do; as the broken tools of a distorted religion, they will enrich a distorted fertility and produce marvelous crops of thorns and thistles. The word pair "thorn and thistle" occurs only here and in Gen. 3:17, where it is part of the judgment on Adam. It is difficult not to see more than accident in this fact and read this as yet another way of emphasizing that the salvation history is at an end. Israel is back with Adam under the curse.

The cry to the mountains, "Cover us," and to the hills, "Fall upon us," is no simple death wish; it is a statement about the alternative. To be crushed to the death by falling rocks is a fate one would not choose; but, says the prophet, it is so much better than what God has in store that it becomes desirable, something to be prayed for. The theme of death as a grace is also limited as in Hos.

9:6, where we also find nettles and thorns. The thorns and thistles of Gen. 3:17 just referred to are also followed by the promise of death and the prohibition of eternal life — presumably because death is preferable to everlasting life for those in a state of sin. Again we have the theme of death as grace.

TUMULT OF WAR (10:9-15)

As with Hos. 10:1-8 there are reasons for treating these verses as a unity. One of these is shared with the first half of the chapter: both begin and end with references to "Israel." Further support for unitary treatment is that 10:8 is a clear end and 11:1 very obviously a new beginning. Therefore at one time 10:9-15 was transmitted as one unit. This is not to make a claim about time or place of origin. The verses divide into at least three subsections, and these may well have appeared at times widely separated. That is a minor matter. We receive them in their present order with a marked beginning and a marked end. What of the middle? Is there a discernible pattern which moves with theological cohesion from beginning to end? I believe there is and that in following the pattern we add to, rather than detract from, the weight of the individual parts.

The pattern is one which begins in war (vv. 9-10) and ends in war (vv. 14-15), but the war now has changed. It has grown, and what starts with battle ends with overtones of the last battle. In between is a theological rationale for this martial development presented to us in agricultural terminology of a remarkably varied nature (vv. 11-13); hardly anything from plowing and sowing to reaping and eating is omitted. It is agricultural but not pastoral; it is intensely theological and historical. The passage is historical as well as theological, because in combination with vv. 9-10 and 14-15 we have the bones of Israel's history. A beginning in sin and internal strife was followed by the adoption of an agricultural way of life which at first was idyllic (v. 11a-c; cf. 9:10; 10:1) but later turned via unrighteousness to educational punishment (10:11d-f) and to a call for repentance (v. 12). This call was not heeded (v. 13a-c) and so led finally to the war that ended the history.

10:9-10   Whatever was intended in 9:9 must be our starting point here, as we must assume that the phrase "the days of Gibeah" has a basic meaning common to both verses. In commenting on 9:9 we opted for the earlier of two possible periods, that is, the events recorded in Judg. 19–21 rather than the kingship of Saul (1 Sam. 10:26; 11:4). This historical background to the two mentions of Gibeah makes most sense of what follows. Indeed, the Judges account is not only one of lust and violence; it is also about warfare, and warfare that leaves one tribe decimated and Israel sadly wounded. It is not too difficult to see the parallels between Gibeah in Judg. 19–21 and what Hosea knew and expected in his own times. Gibeah, like other historical references in the prophecy, is both symbol and force, and more was involved than a vague belief that "history repeats itself." For Hosea, to speak in such terms—as though there were a power called "history"—would no doubt have been verging on idolatry. What was the "force" of Gibeah? I offer three suggestions as to how ancient events became determinators of the present. They are not severally exclusive; all three contribute something to our understanding.

1. Just as the personality of Jacob (or Abraham, or Ephraim) continued in and influenced his successors, so there appears to be a "corporate" influence and power which arose in certain events and which never ceased to agitate and in part to control later events. The supreme example in the OT is the Exodus, whose "force" was always just beneath the surface of history, ready to give direction and power to later times.

2. There is at work another process, which is similar to the influence of events and perhaps even identical, wherein origins tend to become principles or patterns. The word "principles" illustrates the process; it comes itself from a word which means "beginning." The confusion over the meaning of "original sin" also throws light on the process. Is original sin the "historical" sin of Adam, or is it something that is at the root of all we do; in other words, is there a principle of sin? Or is it both? That is, is it an origin which is also a "principle"?

3. The third and most obvious suggestion is of course that the continuity between past and present is accounted for by the fact that history, especially Israel's history, is the activity of God—his footprints in the sand of time—and that some of the patterns in Israel's affairs reflect the consistency of God.

The three phrases in the RSV translation of Hos. 10:9 summarize the entire section. The first speaks of Israel as a "days-of-

Gibeah" nation: a sinful nation given to war. The third phrase, "shall not war overtake them in Gibeah," corresponds to vv. 14-15. The middle, "there they have continued," gives the nucleus of at least 12:1. The original sense of the word "continued" means to remain unmoved and unchanged, the very opposite of making the turn and returning that is demanded of Israel. This is identical with vv. 12 and 13. Verse 12 once more offers Israel the opportunity to change their ways and seek the LORD—in other words, not to continue there (in Gibeah?) but to return. The offer is not accepted, "therefore the tumult of war shall arise among your people."

10 This verse amplifies the "overtaking" war (v. 9). First, the war is God himself coming against the "sons of wrongdoing." Second, it is the nations gathering against them. This, of course, is not two enemies on two fronts; it is God through the nations chastising his people. Just as the evil of Benjamin was punished at Gibeah by God using the other tribes, so at this latter-day Gibeah God uses the nations to punish Israel. Israel is punished because they have misused their freedom and sinned; the nations are used as an instrument of God's chastisement without the option to obey or disobey. The two relationships are utterly different: one is personal and the other wholly impersonal. This divergence is everywhere in the OT in one form or another and need not be discussed here. The only reason for this mention is to remark on how the distinction is taken for granted—it is essential to all the rest—and not commented on. A distinct "saving history" which at times is a "doom history" is not questioned; it is a "given" which underlies all else.

The "double iniquity" has prompted much speculation, and one commentary offers a dozen solutions from which to choose. My guess is that it is either a form of emphasizing the iniquity, on the simple principle that two wrongs are worse than one, or that the "two iniquities" are the original sins at Gibeah and their modern counterparts.

10:11-13c These lines are united by the profusion of farming imagery and vocabulary. Out of fifteen printed lines or partial lines in the RSV, thirteen include distinctive agricultural terms. Much is being implied. As indicated above we have here both history and theology, but also there are cultural and cultic overtones. This is because the culture became an agricultural one, and the cult was greatly affected by the religious influences which were common in contemporary agricultural societies. All this is in general. In particular, Hosea is continuing an election tradition which lies behind 9:10 and 10:1. In the beginning Ephraim (or perhaps all Israel) was chosen because the LORD loved him (Deut. 4:3-6, 37). The image in the two earlier quotations was of the vineyard; we have now moved into God's farmyard. Ephraim as a heifer was commendable. He was trained, presumably to thresh, and was happy in his work. He was blessed with a fair neck, perhaps because the work did not require the use of yoke. The picture is of a servant people chosen for its suitability to perform tasks which delighted both master and servant. Then comes the first stage in the great reversal: the soft life of the favorite comes to an end. Instead of slowly treading the corn and eating its fill meanwhile, the heifer is yoked to the plow and harrow. All parts of Israel—Ephraim, Judah, and Jacob—are like racehorses now forced to pull a coal cart. We are shown a contrast between pampered gentility and hard labor, but the two descriptions are both of work. The election in Hosea's tradition was for service, whether it was pleasant and satisfying or harsh and burdensome.

The farmyard models continue in Hos. 10:12, but the tale changes. Past and future tenses are left behind, and imperatives take over which introduce a new set of values. No longer is it a question of whether the job is easy or unpleasant; the whole business of agricultural and cultural realms is relegated to second or third place. The foremost place is given to "how stand you with God?" To plow and sow and reap and mow are not unimportant; they are essential to life, but they cannot have first priority. Israel's first priority is their relationship with God. While maintaining the same farming vocabulary, words belonging to the covenant are introduced. Israel must "sow righteousness," "reap the fruit of steadfast love" (*ḥesed*), "seek the LORD," and expect the "rain of salvation." Righteousness is the behavior which keeps covenant sweet, healthy, and intact. Steadfast love is the love that flows from faithfulness to the covenant and which in turn promotes the righteousness that preserves the covenant. "Salvation" is what God does for his covenant people and corresponds both linguistically and theologically to the righteousness which is demanded of Israel. The combination of the two vocabularies—the farmyard and the covenant—adds up to what the NT means when it says "Seek first his kingdom and his righteousness, and all these things shall be yours as well" (Matt. 6:33). The produce of the flock and field are God's gifts which come to those who keep covenant with God and thus are still on offer. The whole tenor of Hos. 10:12 is that it is not too late, there is yet time to turn and return, "for it is the time to seek the LORD." The offer is made but is not accepted, as the following verses show.

10:13-15   If 10:13-15 was originally an independent oracle, it was chosen and combined with vv. 9-12 because (1) it continues the farming images and (2) it returns to the subject of warfare with which the section begins. Instead of sowing righteousness, reaping the fruit of steadfast love, seeking the LORD, and enjoying the rain of salvation, the people have plowed iniquity, reaped injustice, and eaten the fruit of lies. The correspondences between v. 12 and the first half of v. 13 are such that it is preferable to accept that these at least originated together. The larger question begins with the second half of v. 13.

The objects of the verbs in vv. 13a, b, c—"iniquity," "injustice," "the fruit of lies"—are the opposite of righteousness, steadfast love, and salvation in the sense that they represent forms of behavior that destroy the covenant relationship, whereas righteousness, steadfast love, and salvation are either covenant builders or the fruits of covenant. So much is clear. What is less clear is how iniquity, injustice, and the fruit of lies relate to each other and to the second part of the verse. I see three questions which must be asked:

1. Are the three phrases of vv. 13a, b, c three ways of saying more or less the same thing? Is this a cumulative statement about Israel's sins in which iniquity, injustice, and the fruit of lies are used almost as synonyms and the plowing, reaping, and eating are merely appropriate verbs to go with the objects in question? Or do we see a progress, a development of thought, as the verbs certainly suggest—you first plow and then reap and finally eat?

2. If we follow the RSV version, the second half of v. 13 begins with "because." This means that what follows "because" is a reason for something else happening. Is the "something else" the activities in v. 13a-c, or is it the contents of vv. 14-15? Either appears to be possible.

3. Some translations omit the "because," which leaves open the

possibility that v. 13d, e, about trusting chariots and warriors, is not there to provide a reason or cause at all, but is merely a member in a list of Israel's wrongdoings. That is, just as the people have plowed iniquity, reaped injustice, and eaten the fruit of lies, so they have trusted in chariots and warriors.

In the interpretation of vv. 12 and 13a-c we have noted that behind all the varied terms is concern with Israel's covenant relationship with Yahweh. No matter whether Israel was being told to sow righteousness and reap the fruit of steadfast love or alternatively was being rebuked for plowing iniquity, reaping injustice, and eating the fruit of lies, the real subject is the state of the covenant. If the covenant lies behind so much else, then might it not also provide the clue to our three questions? I believe that it does. The crucial phrase is v. 13c, "because you have trusted in your chariots. . . ," and the relevant word is "trusted." It implies the thing or person in which you find your security; Israel found it in their numerous chariots and in their well-trained commandos. This is not only a statement about Israel and their armed forces; far more significantly it is a statement about Israel and Yahweh. If Israel puts their trust in the forces of the crown, then they are not trusting in God. This therefore is a statement about covenant. Israel faced with crisis has made the choice between military force and God, and God has lost out. The covenant has been broken, and all sin broke loose as detailed in v. 13a-c. But not only did sin break loose; all punishment broke loose in the form of "tumult of war," with all its horrors. The "because" of v. 13d seems to account for v. 13a-c and for all that follows after in vv. 14 and 15. The turning from God has brought a moral and religious harvest and finally a social and political one. Israel had taken the sword and therefore would perish by the sword, an inevitable movement but one not confined to the moral plane. The reality is shown to be much more complex, as the process is more religious and theological and turns on the nature of Israel's trust or faith.

The reference to Shalman's destruction of Beth-arbel has given rise to numerous suggested dates and identifications. It could refer to Shalmaneser V (727-722 B.C.) or a Moabite king Salamaner or someone unknown to us. The identification is not too important in the light of vv. 10 and 15a, b. The latter citation shows that the decision is Yahweh's and gives the reason, "your great wickedness." The point is strengthened by v. 10: "I will come against the wayward people to chastise them; and nations shall be gathered against them . . ." The identity of the enemies or of Shalman is therefore secondary. The nations may "be gathered against them," but the operative phrase is "I will come . . ." Yahweh decides; Yahweh acts; Yahweh punishes; Yahweh is the enemy.

The section is "determined" in part by the "days of Gibeah," and we have chosen to understand the expression against the background of sin and warfare recorded in Judg. 19–21. The chosen context has served us well until the latter part of Hos. 10:15: "In the storm (or 'dawn,' 'morning'—with the Hebrew text, even 'one fine morning') the king of Israel shall be utterly cut off." The reference to the king at least raises the question as to whether the other "days of Gibeah" (i.e., when Saul the first king lived in Gibeah) could have been intended. In response to a likely protest that it is impossible to "have it both ways," one must say that in this case it is perfectly possible to have it both ways, or even three or four ways. What would "the days of Rome" mean? Or "the days of Oxford"? Would "the days of Paris" limit one to the time of the French Revolution or of the 19th cent. Impressionists, or to 1968, and so forth? Symbols are rarely imprisoned in one definition. They may at any one time serve a particular cause by focusing on a fragment of their long histories; but even then the long history is still there, and rays of light can emanate from any part of it. In the prophecy about the king in v. 15, therefore, we see a reflection of the monarchical aspects of Gibeah's history. As Israel's first king, who had displeased God and his prophet, died tragically in time of war and was "utterly cut off," so will Israel's last king likewise perish.

THE WHOLE STORY:
THE CENTRAL THEME
RESTATED
Hosea 11:1-11

Several references to ch. 11 have already appeared in this Commentary, especially in the Introduction and in the first three chapters. I shall try to avoid repetition in what follows of what has already been said, but a little may be unavoidable. The reasons I have crossed this particular bridge before reaching it are twofold. First, I have assumed that the chapter must be accorded some priority. It is the clearest statement of Hosea's central theme and as such provides a clue to the interpretation of the rest of the book. It also gives a convenient summary of the book's message. Second, I am confident that here we penetrate deeper into the heart and mind of God than anywhere else in the OT. Read aright (a most difficult task) and supplemented perhaps by Isa. 52:13; 53:12, this chapter takes us as near to the Father as it is possible to get without the direct leading of the incarnate Son. Like the Isaiah passage it announces what is the central biblical message of judgment/mercy, bondage/Exodus, destruction/construction, chaos/recreation, death/life, cross/resurrection, to name but some of the most prominent ways in which its central message may be expressed. It is the message of descent from greatness followed by an ascent to comparable or even greater greatness. This dominant scriptural motif has been called the "U" pattern because of the descent and ascent. The Hosea and Isaiah passages both exemplify it and at the same time point to the NT where the model is everywhere, but nowhere more perfectly presented than in Phil. 2:5-11. There Jesus (like the suffering servant) is hymned as descending, suffering, dying, and then rising to glory.

I have chosen to link this chapter to Hos. 8–10 because it is marked by the same emphasis on Israel's history. As it tells the whole story of that history from beginning to restored conclusion, it can be regarded as rounding off the section with a summary of the history and doctrines it reveals. However, not everyone agrees with this division. Hans Walter Wolff, for example, stresses the destructiveness of the chapter (*Hosea,* 203-4); others see even closer links with chs. 12–14. The division is in fact arbitrary and certainly not of crucial importance. Of much greater import is how to translate the very difficult text of the chapter. Some mention will be made below of major problems in translation while bearing in mind that the RSV version must remain the norm in this particular Commentary.

There is no adequate reason for excluding or bracketing 11:10 on the grounds that it alone is in the third person, so I propose to treat vv. 1-11 as a unity. The pericope divides into four parts: vv. 1-4, 5-7, 8-9, 10-11; moreover I applaud James M. Ward when he remarks that "The poem comprises four highly impressionistic pieces, set one after another without narrative transitions. This feature is a stroke of genius and not a mark of its disunity . . ." (*Hosea,* 194).

11:1-4   Israel's history begins with election, an election out of bondage because of God's love. Historically Israel's beginning was with the Exodus, which like every specific event had long roots in the past; but theologically the beginning was in love and in election. Israel would have had no existence without God's love and God's choosing. But this was no "love-child," where the "love" only accounts for the origin of the child; Israel's whole existence— present and future as well as past—depended on God's continuing love and the perpetual election expressed in Covenant. The chosen people live forever only with the patient, long-suffering love of God. The whole prophecy bears witness to this truth.

Israel's birth was an adoption. Sonship was conferred on an existing "child" (or "youth" or "lad"), someone perhaps in his teens but still dependent. Hosea as usual is drawing on the central kerygma of the OT, that is, the gospel of the Exodus. But what he says also accords with the earlier foreshadowing of this good news in Genesis. Abraham too was adopted. He, like the later Israel, was not made for the task; both of them were chosen and called out of the world of the nations. Their pre-election origins were not special; they were children of Adam before they were children of God. They were born again, not of the flesh, not of the will of mankind, but of God's love and election. In this gospel a greater gospel is prefigured: "mission and redemption are in the air," for what is possible for Abraham and Israel is possible with the nations from which they emerge.

So much for some of the early roots of Hosea's statements. Are other parts of the tradition brought to mind? God the father and Israel the son are not metaphors which are exclusive to Hosea. They are found in Isaiah and Jeremiah, and more significantly in Exod. 4:22: "And you shall say to Pharaoh, 'Thus says the LORD, Israel is my first-born son, and I say to you, "Let my son go that he may serve me."'" But perhaps most notable in relation to understanding the chapter are the regulations regarding rebellious sons in Deut. 21:18-21. On the accusation of a son by his parents, the city elders shall stone him to death with stones; "so you shall purge the evil from your midst; and all Israel shall hear, and fear."

There follows, beginning with Hos. 11:2, the story of a rebellious and prodigal son. What is to happen to such a son? How will the story end? These would be nonquestions if the parent is prepared to make an indictment. Everyone knew precisely what the outcome should be; the procedure and purpose and conclusion had all been laid out in the law—God's law. And in this story the parent indicts in no uncertain terms. Strictly speaking there should be no real story here, only the report of a common court case and the inevitable execution. The facts, however, are very different. Perhaps we understand them better and wonder at them all the more if we are prepared to accept that the narrative is in silent dialogue with the law and that ultimately the verdict is contrary to it.

The rebellion is emphasized by contrasting it with God's love and election. God says "come," and like Jonah they go. Not only do they separate themselves from him, but they answer to the call of the Baals and the idols. Theirs is not only a policy of avoidance; it is a positive policy of attachment to the gods of the land. Here there is the hint of a principle. Not only does nature abhor a vacuum; the same is true of supernature. To separate from God is automatically to be separated to idols. The atheist is an impossibility. All people are people of faith, and all that is in question is the object of faith.

This chapter has much in common with ch. 2, but there appears to be one great difference between them. Whereas ch. 2 assumes an early period of faithfulness—a brief honeymoon of obedient and loving friendship — the present chapter sounds more like

Ezekiel's later view (Ezek. 16, 20, 23) and allows for nothing but rebellion from the beginning.

Hosea 11:3 and 4 continue (in the RSV translation) the image of the child (except for v. 4d). The Hebrew text reads "yoke." If another vowel is read (with the LXX), and many would follow this reading, the phrase is "and I became to them as one who lifts a baby to their cheeks," thus presenting the same image throughout. But either way God's loving care and protection is obviously the point that is being stressed. Contrasted with this is Israel's lack of the knowledge of God's concern: "but they did not know that I healed them." No doubt the implication is not that they were utterly ingratiate, but that, just as they sacrificed to the Baals and burnt incense to idols, so they offered God their thanks.

The clear references in v. 1 to Egypt, to God's calling, and to Israel's youth permit one to ask whether vv. 3 and 4 are not an impressionistic description of the wilderness wandering. After all, Exod. 15:26 does speak of God as Israel's healer (Hos. 11:3). If the original context of the verses was the wilderness, then the learning to walk (v. 3) and the being led (v. 4) can be understood against this background. The healing (v. 3) can point to the salvific fact of the Exodus itself or to the divine Doctor's protective love on the journey, and the feeding (v. 4) may recall the manna and the quails. This should not be stressed and is not too significant anyhow. Whatever was the earthen vessel of the original historical container, the religious content is plain and enduring. It obviously spoke to Judah from the time v. 12 was written, up to whenever the Prophets were canonized and beyond that into the era of the Church. God is always seeking to teach, to protect, to heal, to pity, to love, to feed his children.

11:5-7 How "fraught with background" and heavy with meaning is the declaration "They shall return to the land of Egypt." If, as has been suggested, much of this chapter is in dialogue with Deut. 21:18-21, then Hos. 11:4 starts with the assumption that the law is absolute and that the divine lawgiver is wholly obedient to his own law. The rebellious son must die; he must return to the soil from which he was taken. Therefore Israel must return to the place from which they were taken — the place of bondage and death. There must be punishment to fit the crime.

Much else, however, is being implied. In order to discover some of the implications we might ask what is being emphasized. Would Hosea have stressed the word "shall" or the word "return" or the word "Egypt"? A stressed "shall" means that there has been much previous cogitation. God has been weighing the pros and cons of the case for a long time; now finally he shouts out his final decision: "They *shall* return . . ." An emphasis on "return" could imply that God has been musing on the Exodus and on the miseries Israel had known in bondage and from which he had saved them. But all the grimness and horror notwithstanding, it shall be as though the Exodus had not taken place. "They shall *return* . . ." "Return" also points to the end of v. 5 and other parts of the chapter where Israel's refusal to return to God is condemned. If they will not return to their healer and to the source of their being, they shall return somewhere else, and that shall be to Egypt rather than to God — to death rather than to life. And what if Hosea with a rising scream of incredulity heard God shouting the word "Egypt"? This could mean that he was thinking not only of his own decision that they should return, but that his decision was made in the light of their own decision to "return" to Egypt, that is, to appeal to Egypt for salvation and security in the face of present threats.

Such an understanding underlines Israel's complete inability to learn from the past—Jacob had turned to Egypt for help and see what resulted! It also highlights a blindness which is beyond imagining. Faced with a choice between the God who saved them from bondage and a return to that bondage, they choose the latter. Thus the choice of death rather than life is first of all Israel's choice. The people have not only opted out of their vocation as the chosen people and voted to return to being among the nations. They have deliberately chosen to be a slave in the concentration camp of Egypt from which they had been saved.

The linking of Egypt with Assyria results in a slight paradox which is theologically significant. It is almost certain that the mention of these nations reflects very specific diplomatic moves taken by Israel in the decade or more before the nation's eventual downfall. The commentaries are not entirely agreed either on the year or the events referred to, but there is general agreement that clear historical happenings stand behind these three verses. In other words, the God of Israel is speaking in and through the concrete facts of Israel's history, as was his wont. At the same time the juxtaposition of Egypt and Assyria in v. 5a, b and what is said about them takes us beyond the purely historical and leads us into the wider domains of symbol and theology. The historian in us asks how Assyria can be Israel's king if they are back in Egypt; the answer is that "he" cannot be unless Assyrian domination of Egypt is part of the prophetic message, and this is rather unlikely. The theologian in us sees in the verse what is everywhere in Scripture —the general enfolded in the particular, the enduring and eternal incarnate in the passing and the temporal. The verse has come down to us not for the historical reference but for the unchanging truth the reference bears.

Detailed discussion of the translation difficulties encountered in vv. 6 and 7 do not belong in this commentary. A glance at other commentaries or even other translations will show that we are dealing with expressions which resist clear interpretation. A common feature of the various translations is, however, that in these verses God continues to accept the verdict propounded in Deuteronomy. The law applies to the rebellious. Israel and God are intent on punishment and even destruction. The compassion evident in Hos. 11:1-4 and 8ff. is entirely absent in vv. 4-7. The God of goodness and severity shows only his severity and leaves out his goodness. Certainly in the RSV translation there is no preparation whatsoever for what appears in vv. 8ff. This represents Hosea at his most condemnatory and God at his most legal. The sword shall rage and consume and devour because of Israel's rebellion, which is deliberate and intended (vv. 5c, 7a); the yoke is to be fixed permanently, never to be lifted (v. 7c).

11:8-9   To the dialogue with the Deuteronomic law is now added a far more significant dialogue—the dialogue of God with himself in which law and grace, goodness and severity do battle. Other places in the OT speak of God repenting, and elsewhere he is recorded as changing his mind, but nowhere else is there such an awesome unveiling of his own inner conversation. Here is the legitimizing of all dialogue. Here is a clue to biblical interpretation, with its suggestion that God's word in Scripture must be heard as a parliament if God's own self-consciousness includes a "government" and "his Majesty's opposition." Here is the foreshadowing of the trinity. But here also is ineffable mystery. We dare to eavesdrop on God only if we have a proper fear and are fully aware that even the best tuned ear will mishear and the finest mind misunderstand.

The theme that the mercy of God will always triumph over his severity is in a sense a return to the mood of vv. 1-4. On the other hand, it is quite unexpected, and in the light of vv. 5-7 it comes with the shock that any great reversal produces. Perhaps the startling nature of the affirmation is deliberately underlined by the change to direct address, as four times in v. 8 the father speaks *to* the son after only speaking *of* him in vv. 1-7. The first and second times he says "you" God uses names from vv. 1 and 2. The love, leading, and caring of Ephraim/Israel alluded to in these verses are being recalled, and the legal verdict of vv. 5-7 is being questioned and transcended both by the content of the words and their grammatical form. When for the third and fourth times God says "you," it is in association with Admah and Zeboiim, two places always linked with Sodom and Gomorrah (Gen. 10:19; 14:2, 8; Deut. 29:22-23) and like them symbols of evil and deserved destruction. Here it is not the similarity between Admah and Zeboiim on the one hand and Ephraim/Israel on the other that is being announced. Rather, God is declaring his utter inability to treat the firstborn son as he had these cities of the plain. The rebel against the law is now not Israel but the heart of God as it recoils within him. This response of the heart, which in OT parlance includes the mind and the will, is paralleled by God's compassion. Thus the emotions fuel God's thoughts and deliberations, which in turn engender the decision to act against the plain meaning of the law and the dictator of his own standards of justice.

Four times in Hos. 11:8 God says "you" to his son as he bares his soul for mankind to see his tenderness and vulnerability. He also intends to let them glimpse a new law that transcends the old law and a new logic that lies beneath the canons of the old. Then in v. 9, as though to balance and complete the four "you's," God thunders four negatives. He will *not* execute his fierce anger; he will *not* again destroy Ephraim; he is *not* human but God; and then finally, to underline and summarize, God repeats that he will *not* destroy.

11:10-11   There is more still to be said about vv. 8 and 9; but as their interpretation cannot be separated from the succeeding prophecy, we must first examine that and then return to the earlier verses. There is a radical, almost violent change as we pass from v. 9 to v. 10. Grammatically we move from first to third person, both singular and plural; metaphors of compassion give way to lions; the apparently vacillating God becomes imperial and utterly in control; and from God's inner dialogue in the present we shift to Israel's eschatological future. Yet despite the surprising change of scene, the drama is the same, and we find we are in the last act which throws light on the earlier ones.

The father of vv. 1-4 who led Israel out of Egypt has become a lion, but he is still leading his people. What is more, he is still leading them out of Egypt in order to settle them once more in their old lands. The motif of leading is not the only one typical of what has gone before. In 5:14 God is likened to a lion. The images of sonship, birds, doves, return, as well as the pairing of Egypt and Assyria all belong to Hosea's stock in trade. Old themes are made to serve the old promise of a second Exodus and a second entry into the Promised Land, and the chapter ends (11:11 is the final verse in the Hebrew text) with the eschatological hope couched in an oracle from God, "I will return them to their homes, says the LORD."

Now that we have read the story to the end, what can be said in further elucidation of some of the more obscure references of the earlier part of the narrative? Does God's refusal to execute his fierce anger mean that the legal verdict is swept aside and the punishment withdrawn? If so, what does this mean for the authority of the law, and what does it say about God's consistency and integrity? Is God a vacillating God at the mercy of his feelings? What is meant by the affirmation that God is God and not human? Does this mean that it is divine to allow the feeling of compassion to overrule a sense of justice, or does it mean the opposite as some maintain? And how does the declaration of God's divinity over against his possible humanity relate to the assertion that God is the Holy One in their midst? Is there really a new law transcending the old, and is it true that our usual logic is established on the hidden infrastructure of reason that Aristotle never knew?

Most of the answers to these questions must find their starting point in vv. 10 and 11 and their tale of what the future holds. Israel will follow after the LORD (and therefore not after the Baals and the idols) when he leads them from Egypt and Assyria. This of course means that the people were in Egypt and Assyria or they couldn't have been led out, and this in turn means that the verdict was not swept aside and that the punishment happened even as the law prescribed. But if so, then why all the fuss and why God's anguish and the pain of his own private civil war? And if the law was allowed to run its course, how then did God differ from just people and true whose integrity also depended on being law-abiding? The clue lies in the nature of the punishment and whether the punishment was the last word or was only a stage in the process of God's dealing with his people.

In vv. 8 and 9 God is considering a punishment which would be the last word. The law demanded capital punishment, and the verbs in v. 8a, b and the comparison with Admah and Zeboiim in v. 8c and d made it certain that what God's heart recoils against is a verdict which is terminal. This is confirmed in v. 9 with its double refusal to destroy. The inner struggle is not over "to punish or not to punish" but over the finality of the punishment. What the law demanded was indeed final—death by stoning is a very terminal illness! Death is as final as one can get, unless one is God who is the source of life. This explains the affirmation of divinity in v. 9. Whether it is God or mankind, justice demands that the verdict stands; it must not be gainsaid or tampered with. Here God and mankind are equal. Where the difference lies is that for humans death is the end, but for God it is the very source of life, in that there is life beyond death. This surely is the explanation of v. 9c, d, where the essential difference between God and mankind is emphasized and God's utter dissimilarity made doubly plain by rooting all in the unique language used to describe his utter uniqueness —"the Holy One in your midst." The Holy One is the source of justice and love—hence the conflict in v. 8. But the Holy One is also the Creator and Re-creator, the fount of life—hence the solution. Justice demands the verdict and the execution, but love is satisfied in restoration, in renewal, in resurrection; thus it is a resurrected Israel that is being pointed to. Just as there was a re-wooing and re-marriage in the early chapters of Hosea, so there is a new beginning envisaged when the image changes to sonship.

Have the questions above all been answered? Some have. The verdict was not ignored, and the punishment took place. The law remains inviolate, unscathed. But what about God? Is he proved to be inconsistent? He is indeed proved to have a share in mankind's divided loyalties to justice and mercy. But he is shown to be true to both in ways that mankind cannot be, and he is shown, if words like "bias" are permitted, to maintain his bias on the side of mercy. Thus we are shown that the very core of holiness is love, and that justice is the handmaid of mercy and a stage on the way to love's fulfillment.

Two questions remain unanswered. Is there indeed evidence of a new law and a new logic revealed in the conflict of v. 8, the affirmations of v. 9, and the prophecies of vv. 10 and 11? I believe so, although both are as old as God himself. For human law and logic destruction is destruction, death is final, and ends are ends. Within such a world of clear conclusions, syllogisms and the observable law of cause and effect are at home and adequate. Hosea however is pointing to a new world where destruction is a challenge, death an opportunity, and ends are beginnings and places of hope. In other words, he is assuming that some graves have lives beyond them because the living God is beginning to show to his people that he is a God of resurrection and life; he is showing that this view changes all things, including the very foundations of thought. The old human law and human logic are being both fulfilled and transcended by the incursion of eternity into human life. God is indestructible, he does not die, and he has no end. Thus here his life is showing signs, in the "midst of" Israel's life, of taking over. Israel must suffer, die, and be destroyed, but this "end" is not final. Israel will be reborn or resurrected because, of all mankind, only Israel has the Holy One "in the midst," giving them a share of God's own nature. The old law and the logic of cause and effect spelled the end for Israel in their world of clear conclusions. But a new world is beginning to appear where there is no conclusion, clear or obvious, because it is the world of the everlasting God. As in 2:19, Israel's future is grounded in this new world. All unknowing, Hosea is glimpsing the Father not only of Israel but of the One who could say, "I am the resurrection and the life."

SECTION IV

PAST, PRESENT, AND FUTURE: ON TO THE KNOWLEDGE OF GOD

FATHERS AND SONS
Hosea 11:12–12:14

The Hebrew text, which is certainly correct in this matter, begins ch. 12 with our 11:12. We shall follow this arrangement while retaining the verse numbers of the RSV. Unfortunately, commendation of the Hebrew text can go no further. In an obscure book, nothing is more obscure than the present chapter. Questions abound everywhere about almost everything, and the temptation is to make our comments brief and to pass over quickly to remaining chapters, lest time be wasted speculating further on a speculative translation of a speculative original. Not surprisingly, previous commentators exhibit a considerable variety in what they write. But quite surprisingly, several of them find grounds for treating the chapter as a unity, even though the reasons adduced are not the same. For some the unifying factors are linguistic, for some thematic, and for some the cohesion lies in the literary form. This constitutes a challenge: to discuss the unity, if at all possible, and to make it speak theologically to our day.

According to our plan for dividing the book, ch. 12 stands at the beginning of the fourth and final section, which culminates in the hopeful ch. 14, with which the book ends. Much of what has gone before can be described as a dialogue with the past and particularly with the era of the Exodus, which so far has been taken as the starting point of Israel's life with Yahweh. It has been the Exodus and a few of the succeeding events in Israel's history which have provided the raw material for judging the present and also contributed models for anticipating the future as Hosea looks longingly for a second Exodus. Nothing earlier than the Exodus has yet appeared. Suddenly, as we near the end, Hosea reaches back into the patriarchal period, and the dialogue is now made to include Jacob the individual—the father of Israel. How these patriarchal references are made to function is a puzzle. Is there an intended contrast between

153

the father-son relationship of ch. 11 and the very different relationship existing between Jacob and his descendants, or is the explanation to be found not in a preceding chapter but in ch. 14? But what
possible relationship could there be between the hopeful future and
a distant past marked by deceit and lies? We have noted above that,
as in the physical world every action has its corresponding reaction,
so in the spiritual world there is often an affinity of opposites: the
further you go in one direction the further you are propelled in the
opposite direction. Could it be that, in preparation for advance into
the joyous idealism of ch. 14, the beginning of the section needs to
include a retreat into the ambiguous realism of the days of Jacob?
Few things in the book are more unclear than the Jacob references;
nothing is more challenging.

I am borrowing a suggestion of James M. Ward, who sees the
chapter consisting of five poems, each one having two parts:

> The first part is an accusation, or sarcastic recollection, con-
> sisting of from two to four lines. The second part is a threat,
> and is always stated in a single line. This last feature of the
> poems is actually the clue to the structure of the chapter. It
> can hardly be accidental that the chapter has one-line threats
> occurring at such regular intervals. Each threat is logically
> dependent upon what precedes it. (*Hosea*, 214)

The five poems are: 11:12–12:2; 12:3-6; 12:7-9; 12:10-11;
12:12-14.

11:12–12:2   The chapter begins with the statement of one of
its major themes—perhaps its major theme: lies and deceit. This
is never far from us, and on the whole it is the lies and deceit of
contemporary Ephraim which are being advertised, as they are in
this primary statement. But who is encompassed? Who is the
"me"? Is it God or is it the prophet Hosea? Whoever it may be is
coupled with "the house of Israel." But which of them is more
likely to be paralleled with "the house of Israel," God or Hosea?
I assume that it is God who is being lied to and deceived, mainly
on the grounds that this is a common theme of the book whereas
the alternative is not.

Another question requiring immediate (if not certain) answer is
about Judah. What precisely is being said about him? The RSV
translates 11:12 so that Judah appears in a favorable light —

"known by God" and "faithful to the Holy One." This however is followed by 12:2, where there is no doubt that Judah is being indicted by God. Do we accept the resulting contradiction or challenge the RSV translation of 11:12? I am compelled to do the latter and retranslate it in such a way that the statement is not favorable to Judah but is exactly the opposite. Judah is linked with Ephraim in lies and deceit, being known by (or "straying after") a Canaanite deity and being faithful to local polytheism or even to the cultic prostitutes. This interpretation of the Hebrew is perfectly possible. Moreover, it removes the contradiction with 12:2 and provides adequate reason for the indictment. Thus the chapter begins with descriptions of the deceit and apostasy of both Ephraim and Judah.

The next verse, 12:1, follows on in the same vein but is restricted to Ephraim's failings. Hosea 11:12 had spoken of Ephraim lying to God in a vain attempt to deceive him. What actually happens is that such insanity only results in Ephraim's own madness growing and his self-deception increasing. Who else but a madman would "herd wind"—or befriend the wind? And this is not any wind but the sirocco, a wind that parches and injures, from which any reasonable individual will take shelter. The wind metaphor is an amplification of the last two phrases. Making treaties with Assyria and Egypt (ratified by oil?) is plain proof of insanity and self-delusion. At best a wind is a nothingness (a vanity of vanities according to Ecclesiastes), but sometimes a wind is much more than mobile emptiness; it is an enemy and a threat. Seeking security from the brutal Assyria and the imprisoning Egypt is like mistaking the death-dealing sirocco for the calm of still waters and the peace of cooling streams. Such behavior draws from God a deserved threat, which is expressed in a triple statement: God will indict, punish, and requite, for he is prosecutor, judge, and executioner.

12:3-6 In v. 2 God's people (or the ten tribes) had been referred to as "Jacob." Hosea now reaches back into the past and examines Jacob's beginnings as recorded in Genesis. The first reference is to Gen. 25:26 and plays upon the meaning of the name. The RSV opts for one meaning, but an alternative translation is "In the womb he tricked his brother," thus continuing and emphasizing the theme of deception and implying that the chosen people have

been named "cheat" since the beginning and are still living up to
their name. The self-willed desire to be "number one" continues
into manhood, and the infant who sought to get the better of his
elder brother in the womb now as an adult tries his strength against
God (Gen. 32:23ff.).

Jacob's competitiveness continues. He fights with a third
protagonist, an angel, and prevails. Who is the angel? Can Genesis
provide any clues? There is, of course, the dream encounter with
angels in Gen. 28, but nothing can be found there to suggest strife.
Is this another reference to the struggle at the Jabbok where the
identity of Jacob's assailant is quite ambivalent, or is Hosea drawing upon traditions which did not achieve canonical status? And
when did Jacob weep and seek an angel's favor as the RSV implies?
If the "angel" refers to Jacob's assailant in Gen. 32, did Jacob use
trickery of which weeping was a part? But Gen. 32 knows nothing
of such maneuvers. It is true that not only does Gen. 33 tell of
Jacob weeping, but the expression "find favor" occurs several times
in the chapter. But what has Esau to do with angels? And also we
must ask whether there is any possible connection between Gen.
32 and 33, since Gen. 32 provides a possible background for Hos.
12:4a with its "angel" and "prevailing" and Gen. 33 provides us
with the "weeping" and "seeking favor" of Hos. 12:4b. Any
answer is a long shot, but there is one that gives the connection we
seek. Rashi, a medieval commentator building on more ancient
rabbinic tradition, identifies Jacob's assailant in Gen. 32 as the
guardian angel of Esau. Did the ancient rabbinic tradition go back
to Hosea, or were Hosea and the rabbis depending on the same
source? It is impossible to say, but Rashi himself by his suggestion
has put Esau (or his angel) into the Gen. 32 narrative, and the
theological complications of this are enormous (see Dow Marmur
Beyond Survival: Reflections on the Future of Judaism [London: Dar-
ton, Longman and Todd, 1982], 3ff.).

The Jacob references continue. God met with Jacob at Bethel
and there God spoke with him. Genesis records two visits of Jacob
to Bethel (Gen. 28:10ff.; 35:1ff.); but God appears only in the
former visit, so presumably Hosea is reflecting that particular one.
What God says is prefixed by Hos. 12:5, which is a doxology and
lends authority to what is said in v. 6. The naming of God as "the
God of hosts" and the emphasis on God's personal name Yahweh
(the Hebrew name by which he is remembered) makes the verse

act like a seal on a document or the signature on a letter. The worth of what is said depends wholly on the nature of the sayer. A threat by a coward or a boaster had only nuisance value; anything from the "God of Armies" must be taken with the utmost seriousness.

Doxologies occur elsewhere in the OT, but most significantly in Amos 4:13; 5:8; 9:5-6. Their function in Amos also appears to be as a seal or signature, and in each instance the doxology is associated with one or more of God's threats or verdicts. In Hos. 5:8 there is also clear association with Bethel. I mention this partly to reinforce the understanding I have of 12:6, because it differs from the RSV. The RSV sees the verse as an appeal to Israel. Supported by Amos's use of doxology and by the pattern of the five poems in the chapter described above, I prefer to take v. 6 as a threat or actual punishment. Ward translates: "So you shall (dwell in your tents), maintaining loyalty and justice, and waiting continually for your God" (*Hosea*, 207). This would coincide with the educative punishment so often referred to in earlier chapters (e.g., 2:6, 7, 9-13; 3:3, 4).

12:7-9   The pattern of this poem is similar to that of the previous one. There is first of all a descriptive condemnation, this time of Ephraim, followed by the "seal" or "signature" stressing God's name and nature. Finally there is the threat or verdict.

In v. 3 the guilt of Ephraim is implicit; in v. 7 it is quite explicit. Although there is no overt mention of the patriarch Jacob, the vocabulary and subject matter imply that he is in the wings if not actually on the stage. The strophe begins with the Hebrew word "Canaan," which had become synonymous for merchant or trade because the Canaanites were famous as travelling salesmen. The word had pejorative overtones in itself, but in case the message was not clear a further phrase was added: "in whose hands are false balances." Finally, for good measure Ephraim's true nature was made doubly clear; he not only oppressed (or cheated, or was treacherous), but he enjoyed it. This was the expression of his essential being. (Jacob by name, Jacob by nature?) The word "Canaan" also carries with it a profound criticism; it strikes, not only at his way of life but at his identity as God's people. Given Canaan as a base for being a holy people and a nation of priests, it was not Canaan that had been sanctified but Ephraim which had been Canaanized, secularized, and corrupted.

As usual, worse follows. The loss of identity is not recognized, and this is demonstrated by a shallow response to deserved criticism. The secularization and corruption do not exist for Ephraim, so something approaching a theological rationale is proposed. Relying on popular theology, he points to his prosperity as proof of his virtue. The argument is the obverse of much of the book of Job and Isa. 53:4 (but resembles Ps. 73:1-12)—riches are the reward of piety as well as of industry. The prophet makes the necessary religious and theological connection that it is not wealth that cleanses guilt, and then becomes the medium of dialogue. Ephraim had said "I am rich"; God's response is brief but heavy with truth and scorn. The great credal statement beginning "I am the LORD" shows Ephraim's defense to be the shameful parody it is. The argument is seen in all its pathetic weakness beside the divine affirmation. But not only is an argument destroyed; Ephraim's existence is revealed as a mere shadow, and it is set in contrast with what it might have been. They had chosen a Canaanite identity when they had been offered identification with the LORD of all being who was prepared, even in their days of shame, to be called "your God." His language is "covenant language" and as such points to what might have been and what Ephraim had in fact made it. Hadn't God redeemed them from the pagan culture of Egypt in order to make them his people, and wouldn't he in turn be their God? Such had been the possibilities. The reality was that they had chosen the role of scheming plunderers and cheats. Now comes the threat. As the Exodus was followed by the wilderness, it is to the wilderness they will be exiled. The reward of their way of life was not riches, which had been secured by oppression and treachery, but their true deserts: nomadic poverty.

12:10-11   The final poem (Hos. 12:12-14) combines and perhaps contrasts the activities of Jacob the natural father and Moses the spiritual father and prophet supreme. It may be that therein lies the main point of the chapter. Jacob and his ways have already been introduced (vv. 3-4); now in preparation for the entry of Moses, the work of the prophets in general is explained in vv. 10-11. First comes their relationship with God, described in the most emphatic way possible, by a triple definition of relationship and function, put into the mouth of God himself: "I spoke . . . I multiplied . . . I gave parables." The prophet is shown to be an extension of God, and the prophetic word and vision are declared to come from God. The main task of the prophet is to speak, but what he speaks is not mere information or even command. Their words relate to the past and the future as well as to the present, but they are neither historians nor fortune tellers. The word they speak creates a new history which judges all other history but at the same time offers it a future and a hope. Israel had been chosen to begin this history and bring its blessings upon the history of the nations. But in order to do this it had to accept the very special identity bestowed by that word of God given to the prophets. This Israel had refused to do. Instead it had chosen a Canaanite identity.

Verse 11 includes two place names, Gilead and Gilgal, which Hosea has already mentioned as places of evildoing (6:8; 9:15). Presumably the evil spoken of is cultic, as the Gilgal reference is followed by allusion to sacrifice and the destruction of altars. It is difficult to comment further on the precise nature of the indictment, as unrecorded contemporary events most likely lie behind what is said. Before we conclude though, it is right to point out that although there is no direct reference to Jacob there may be an allusion to the covenant that he made with Laban in Gen. 31:43ff. and which is marked by a heap of stones and a "heap of witness" (Galeed or Gilead). Ward translates Hos. 12:11 as "But the heap of witness was a fraud! How empty it became: in Gilgal they sacrifice bulls!" (*Hosea*, 208). But these altars will have lost their significance. They will now be only piles of rocks along the furrows of a field.

12:12-14   The final poem continues the pattern of a critical narrative leading up to a threat. The critical narrative (vv. 12 and 13) consists of a comparison of some of Jacob's deeds (v. 12) and the acts of God at the time of the Exodus (v. 13). Central to the latter is the figure of a prophet who can only be Moses. Complete certainty about what is being said escapes us, but some formal aspects are clear. Jacob's acts are for a wife or wives. God's acts are by a prophet ("for" and "by" translate the same Hebrew preposition). The double reference to wives is balanced by a double reference to Moses.

Where Jacob flees the land God brings Israel to it. Where Jacob keeps sheep God keeps Israel, and so forth. The fact of the comparison is clear, but what its purpose is is less clear. Is Jacob under heavy criticism? Are servanthood and shepherding seen as demeaning, especially as they are merely to get a foreign wife (or wives)? Is Israel's love of the fertility rites being attributed to Jacob? Is he asking "What can be expected with such a womanizer for a progenitor?" But if the contrast is between Jacob and God, then why all the emphasis on the prophet Moses? Is the need for mediation the point, or is the prophet used as a symbol for God's word?

There is less doubt about the meaning of v. 14. As in the previous four poems, this one ends (v. 14b, c) with the threat of disaster. The language used, especially "provocation," points to apostasy and idolatry as the major causes of the condemnation and judgment. For Hosea these are capital offences, and the use of the word "bloodguilt" confirms that it is the death sentence that is being passed on God's people.

In the attempt to discern what lies at the heart of the chapter, let us ask, first, what is new in this chapter, and second, what is missing that might be expected, knowing Hosea's major teachings as found in other chapters. We shall begin with what is missing. From the very first chapter of the book, we have found a pattern which might be categorized as "from grace to grace." God gives all to his people, but they rebel; he promises punishment, but the punishment is followed by grace. This pattern is complete in chs. 1, 2, 3 and 11, but parts of it are found everywhere. In ch. 12 the first three elements are found, but only the merest shadows of the final grace can be glimpsed; each of the five poems finishes with punishment but no grace. When we ask what is new in the chapter, we discover that two things qualify: first, the introduction of the patriarch Jacob, and second, the considerable emphasis on the place of the prophets in God's plan, culminating with the supreme prophet, Moses the prophet of the Exodus.

The absence of the redemption motif, so clear in ch. 11, allows us to ask whether ch. 12 is not a part of a greater whole in which its function is to elaborate and expound the nature of the rebellion and the inevitability of the punishment. This I believe is how we should see the chapter—as part of the analysis of both the sin and of the judgment upon the sin. Rebellion and judgment continue in ch. 13, but in ch. 14 comes the redemption which lies beyond the deserved affliction. If this is learned from the absence of grace, what does the presence of Jacob and Moses and all the prophets signify? Do we have to interpret the dual novelty together, or are they distinct and separate, their presence together for the first time being quite fortuitous? If they are to be regarded as independent of each other, then what is Jacob alone saying? Is he there to explain and reinforce the charge against Israel? Does he seek to point out that the Israel of Hosea's day was "a chip off the old block," "like patriarch, like progeny," that evil Jacob could be expected to have evil descendants? Perhaps there is something of this in Hosea's motive, but can it be central? It is not at all certain that Jacob is being depicted as wholly bad. If Hosea had wanted to paint him as completely bad, then there was far better material at hand in Genesis which is not even mentioned. And what is even more surprising is that the parallel between patriarch and progeny breaks down when it comes to the deserved punishment. Jacob dies in his bed full of years and glory with even Egypt mourning him. So it seems we must still keep on looking for the key, and looking in a manner which sees Jacob and prophecy linked in some way. We have looked at Jacob alone; what if we look at the prophetic references alone? When we attempt to do this, we find that they are not really about prophets at all. The prophets (12:10, 13) are only instruments; the two verses are wholly about what God does with the prophets. It is God's behavior we are looking at, not the deeds of the prophets whose sole function is to mediate the words of God (v. 10) and the redemptive acts of God (v. 13). Thus the chapter is about Jacob and his people and about God and his people—two fathers and their sons (to continue the image of ch. 11) and how the fathers relate to their children and how they affect each other.

Jacob is presented not so much as thoroughly evil but as human through and through. He wants his own way and is prepared to do almost anything to get it, even fight with God and angels. He is strong, but he will weep and beg if it suits him. He's like a businessman who says "Business is business" and who looks to his profits as both his security and as proof of his virtue. His values are of this world, and he has become blind to any other. This nature he has bequeathed to his rich blind sons, the Israelites, and they will naturally reap the deserved harvest. And this, implies Hosea, is the real problem, because there is absolutely no natural way out of this natural cycle until it ends naturally in destruction. But there is hope—a supernatural hope which makes its appearance with

Moses at the Exodus. This hope takes the form of a new story (or narrative, or history) which appears alongside the old natural story (or narrative, or history) and exists within it, distinguishable but inseparable. This new story is a saving story designed to change and renovate the old story, and it comes alongside the old story by deed and word; but these are the deeds and words of God, "spoken" into the old story by prophets. The old story resists the new because the latter is a strange and threatening story. The new comes to renew and to heal, but it appears to do the opposite—by coming more as an enemy than as a healer. The old story that leads to eventual destruction appears benign. It gives pleasure, even riches (12:8). It produces little regret, or sense of guilt or remorse (v. 8c, d). It is the new story, the saving history that leads to eventual renewal and redemption, that appears first as severe, harsh, and judgmental, that drives urban capitalists into the wilderness (v. 9), that shatters the places of worship (v. 11), and finally pronounces a dread sentence. The old story makes few demands and is permissive. The new story is very demanding, with an insistent call that Israel should return. Hosea 12 thus presents this meeting of natural and supernatural in the persons of Jacob and the prophets. In it we see the conflict aspect of the meeting. In ch. 14 we see where chs. 12 and 13 are leading—to a time when Israel does return to God and takes to itself words, prophetic words, that make the new story into Israel's own. Then the new story will transform the old, and Israel will dwell beneath God's shadow where it will flourish and blossom.

FROM GRACE TO GRACE
Hosea 13:1-16

Chapter 13 has several links with ch. 12. First, it continues the descent into the pit documented in ch. 12, at the same time gaining momentum as well as depth. Second, it divides into clearly distinguishable sections, which nevertheless have cohesion and form a sequence which is climactic. Also, the first two of the sections have a form which corresponds closely to the pattern in the five parts of ch. 12. Third, the first half of 13:4 is identical with the first half of 12:9. Fourth, ch. 13 takes up, expands, and brings to a terrifying conclusion the great theme of ch. 12: that Israel's identity and security can be found in nothing else but "the LORD their God from the land of Egypt," and when he is not worshipped as savior and healer he becomes judge and destroyer. God is at the same time their source of life and the cause of their death. As the chapter proceeds, hammering home the bad news that God is their enemy, the message and the images that convey it grow ever more immoderate. Two things prevent us from outright resistance to what is said. The first is that the chapter is immediately followed in ch. 14 by the greatest good news for which it mysteriously is the right preparation. Second is the realization that, horrifying as ch. 13 is, its horror is exceeded by the Crucifixion, which also mysteriously is the only preparation possible for the gospel of the Resurrection.

The four sections referred to are 13:1-3, 4-8, 9-14 and 15 and 16. The first two, like those of ch. 12, can be divided each into two parts: a threat of destruction preceded by the reasons therefor.

13:1-3 I have suggested that chs. 12 and 13 are part of a pattern "from grace to grace," describing the fall from grace. This pattern appears in 13:1-3, 4-8 and possibly in 9-14 and 15-16. In both vv. 1-3 and 4-8 an original "grace" is expressed historically by reference to the good old days of the past. In the first three

verses the prophet addresses Ephraim and recollects a time of exaltation when Ephraim could command fear merely by speaking.
It is not clear who precisely is included in the designation
"Ephraim." Is it individual Ephraimites such as Joshua (Josh.
24:30) or Jeroboam I (1 Kgs. 11:26; 12:20)? Or is it the Joseph
tribes? If so, is Hosea saying much the same as Psalm 78, which
deals with the riddle of why the Joseph tribes who began with
every advantage eventually were rejected and had to make way for
Judah? Or is Ephraim here the equivalent to Samaria, which had
wielded great power but is about to be crushed (Hos. 13:16)? No
doubt the answer to such questions was of importance to Hosea's
original hearers, but to later Judah and to the even later canonizers it mattered little. To us it matters even less. In 12:10 we are
instructed that God, through the prophets, gave parables. I take
that to mean that out of their own concrete, very historical events
the prophets distilled a word from the LORD for all years and all
seasons. This word was independent of any exact information
concerning the happenings which gave birth to the parables.
Sufficient is it to know that the people of God were given greatness, but that was a gift which could be spurned. Ephraim spurned
the gift by thanking the Baals, thus repudiating the giver who was
their security, their identity, and their life. Without these they were
as good as dead.

It may be that the reference to Baal in 13:1 refers to Baal-peor
(of 9:10) and that the death is the death incurred there and
recorded in Num. 25. If that was the intention, then the wording
of Hos. 13:2 is a little more understandable because it provides an
explanation of why the people were now sinning more and more
by making for themselves molten images. What does the "more
and more" signify? Why was idol worship worse in the present
than in the past? A possible answer is that a distinction is being
made between joining an existing cult in order to worship idols
made by others and the more deliberate and willful act of making
idols oneself for oneself. It is interesting to note the use of reflexives
of the verb in similar circumstances elsewhere (Exod. 20:4; 32:8;
cf. Hos. 8:4). Is there the implication that, while it is bad enough
to worship other people's idols, it is far worse — almost qualita-
tively worse—to be in the business of producing one's own? Can
it be that the very manufacture of idols is sin of a quite different
order, to be distinguished clearly from adopting the gods of others

—a practice which could be the result of drift or weakness rather than the mark of conscious apostasy.

Just as the chapter develops to a terrifying climax, so do some of its component parts. There may be in 13:2 a build-up of sarcastic irony. The people sin far more than their primitive forefathers because their culture and technology and craftsmanship enable them to make bigger, better, and more beautiful idols than their competitors. Their industry has now prospered: "No need to import consumer goods. We now make everything ourselves. Look, none of your cheap and nasty idols whose heads may drop off. Only the best! Feel the quality! Solid silver and, mind you, made by experts. Oh yes, we're a developed nation." The irony could well continue, only more gruesomely. The RSV follows the Greek version in the last part of the verse. If however we remain with the Hebrew, it is likely that the correct translation is "They say to themselves: 'Those who sacrifice humans kiss calves.'" If this is correct, we need look no further to explain the words "now they sin more and more." What more abominable extension of idol worship could there be than the adoption of human sacrifice which we know was practiced in Israel under certain circumstances? And as though this were not sufficient, insult and mockery are added by the prophet even as the ultimate horror is suggested. Values have become so corrupted and people so blinded by sin that the idols are honored while human life is destroyed. And what idols! Idols in the form of animals! The chain of being has been turned completely upside down. Things and animals are preferred to humans and God. Inanimate idols are put in place of the living LORD, and living people sacrificed to things of metal. A final irony may even be present in the mention of a calf-god which may of course be a representation of Yahweh. This could be part of the climactic effect of this chapter as this verse prepares for vv. 7 and 8. Are we meant to hear God say in his heart "Very well, they have chosen to worship animals; I will respect their choice. But I am no calf to be kissed; I am as lions, leopards, and bears who come to kill."

Ephraim, once exalted, has chosen abasement. In their search for security they have lost their identity. In their worship of "nothings" they have become like the things they reveal—nothing. What follows is punishment — terrible punishment because it is extermination. But at the same time it is almost automatic: God dotting the *i*'s and crossing the *t*'s of Ephraim's own decisions. If despite God's grace, patience, love, and exhortation they insist on becoming nothing, then so be it. They shall be like mist, like dew that disappears with the sun, or the chaff that blows away with the wind. Like smoke up the chimney, they will leave no trace but a black mark.

13:4-8   The descent-into-the-pit pattern is here seen at its clearest, most uncompromising, and most terrible. No greater contrast could be imagined than that between the first two verses and the last two, for the movement is from the grace of election and redemption to the ferocity of being devoured by ravening beasts. But the shift is a logical one and is adequately described in the middle verse, v. 6.

Verse 4 is a divine statement that begins with phrases already used in 12:9. It is covenant language almost identical with the opening words of the Decalogue, and the second half of the verse is the First Commandment in a slightly different form. Its place here in the chapter might be to strengthen further the opposition to idolatry in 13:2-3. Or it might be Hosea's response to Israel's possible protest that God could not destroy them (v. 3) because he was their God and their savior. Whatever the particular reason for repeating it here, the statement is Hosea's central creed. This is his theological, religious, moral, social, cultural starting point. This is where he begins and what he comes back to: election at the time of the Exodus. Even when he intends the horrors of vv. 7-8, this is where he must begin, because for a prophet of Israel there is nowhere else to begin. Israel's history begins here; their raison d'etre begins here; their philosophy begins here. Above all Israel's security, identity, and very existence are inseparable from God's choosing them and saving them out of Egypt. If ever Israel were inclined to ask "Why is there Israel and not no-Israel," the answer could only begin with "I am the LORD your God from the land of Egypt. . ."

The rest of this section follows on with a frightening reasonableness. Israel knew no other God because (1) there was no other God to know, and Israel alone in the world knew that there was no other God and that all the gods were "nothings," and (2) Israel came into existence only because God knew them in a very special way (v. 5) and their existence continued only as long as Israel knew God in return. Without this knowledge of God there was no Israel. Other nations were constituted by race, or geography, or politics, or myth; only one thing constituted Israel and that was knowing the God who first knew them. This God was the source of their being and identity; he was also the guarantee of their security. In the beginning he was their savior from oppression; he nourished them in the wilderness and gave them to drink in days of drought. Their history could well have been a continuation of such protective care. God so willed it, but Israel found God-given security insecure and looked everywhere else for assured protection. She, who was an empress, turned to pimps.

God's gifts became grounds for rebellion. The nurture in the wilderness led on to the gift of land, of milk, honey, vineyard, and pasture. But this was Israel's downfall. The proper response of gratitude, which would have strengthened the knowledge of God and therefore the assurance of security and identity, was not forthcoming. Rather they gave thanks to themselves and to the nonexistent Baals, and finally they forgot God. They travelled the easy road from knowledge to forgetfulness, and as night follows day their doom was sealed; for in their case forgetfulness was not a foible—it was death.

The verb "to know" (vv. 4, 5) is most comprehensive. On God's side it includes election, love, covenant, protection, and security (Amos 3:2); on Israel's side it is all that is involved in being a faithful, obedient, worshipping, holy people. Therefore "knowledge" is the condition of Israel's existence. Without it they are mist, dew, chaff, and smoke. Amazingly this is the destiny they have chosen because they have chosen not to know God. Filled with the good things that come from God's knowledge of them, they have reciprocated by forgetting God (Deut. 8:11-20; 6:10-19; 11:15-16).

The knowledge which Israel has rejected is similar to "faith" where the NT describes the means of appropriating the gifts of God. With Israel's decision to forget God, communications have broken down. The bridges of mercy which carried the privileges of covenant have been severed at Israel's end. The forgetting was an invitation not to communicate, and because Israel's whole existence depended on this communication the result is immediate and drastic. No words could describe it more drastically than those chosen by Hosea. Israel's inversion of the chain of relationships demands something correspondingly shocking. The choice of a calf as an object to worship brings an invasion of wild beasts. The shepherd no longer protects the flock; he has now become the marauder in the form of lions, leopards, and bears, which each in its own natural way proceeds to decimate the flock. God the savior is now the devouring enemy.

13:9-14   The decision to treat these verses together is a difficult one, and good arguments can be advanced for separating them into two or even three divisions. But the grouping of the verses is not that significant an issue, as their place in the whole chapter or even in Section IV (Hos. 11–14) can be defended on grounds of meaning as well as tradition. I incline to regard the verses as a unit because they can also be seen to fit into the pattern which we found in ch. 12 and in 13:1-3, 4-8. Reasons for judgment being passed on Israel are given in vv. 9-13, followed by the pronouncement of sentence in v. 14. The "fall from grace" pattern could be represented quite prominently in these verses as well, if we adopt James M. Ward's translation of vv. 9 and 10. In place of the question found in the RSV, he gives the following rendering: "It is your destruction, O Israel, since your help was in me! I am your king" (*Hosea*, 219). If this is correct, then vv. 9-14 are similar to vv. 1-3 and 4-8. They all begin with reminders of God's gifts in the past before proceeding to give reasons for the threatened destruction with which the passage ends.

Verses 1-3 had shown how the gift of the cult was abused and how it had led to destruction. In vv. 4-8 it was the gift of Canaan that was perverted with fatal results. Now in vv. 9-11 the ambivalent gift of kingship is examined. The accusation was most likely made not long before the siege of Samaria. It may well have as part of its context Shalmaneser V's capture and imprisonment of King Hoshea and some of his courtiers. This would give an historical explanation of the questions in v. 10. Israel may well have been responding to Hosea's gloom-and-doom pronouncement with counterblasts that the king would see that they were kept secure. Now the news has broken that the king was no more, and Hosea is vindicated.

If this is what happened, Hosea is not content just to say "I told you so." He uses the news with devastating effect to reinforce his theological pronouncements and in particular to try to get Israel to believe the unbelievable, namely that no one could help them because God was against them. Verse 9 is the awesome opposite of

St. Paul's question, "If God is for us, who is against us?" In both
cases the answer is plainly "no one." Hosea drives home what
should have been clear long ago, that none of the expected
securities — cult, culture, Canaan, and least of all an imprisoned
king—could be of the slightest use in preparing a defense strategy
against God. Just as the shepherd had joined forces with the wild
beasts, now the helper had become the destroyer. Against God
there is no defense.

Kings and princes dominate vv. 10 and 11. Each line in the
translation refers to them. We are left in no doubt about Hosea's
view of kingship, especially if we see these verses as the culmina-
tion of what has been said in 7:3-7; 8:4-10; 10:3b, 7, 15. From at
least as early as Judg. 9 there exists in the OT a dialogue concerning the worth of kingship and its place in God's plan for his people.
Sympathetic voices saw kingship as an extension of God's
kingship. Those unsympathetic saw the kings as a threat to the
authority and place of God the king. The unsympathetic saw the
kings as part of the general cultural corruption and as something
which God had very reluctantly accepted (1 Sam. 8:6). It is with
this party that Hosea aligns himself in Hos. 13, expressing his
criticism of kings and all their works in the most emphatic terms.
In his own exasperation and anger he attributes the whole business
of kings and court to the wrath of God. Whether God is giving
them kings or removing them, it is from the worst possible mo-
tives. Pedantically, we might protest that God cannot have it both
ways and that v. 11 contains an inner contradiction. If something
is given in anger, then surely its removal is a good thing and not
motivated by wrath. That may be so, particularly if Hosea is dis-
coursing on the theology of government; but he is not. He is talking more about God than about kings. He is saying that God's
patience is exhausted, and that—whether coming or going—kings
are now part of his sinister work of destruction.

In vv. 12 and 13 the direct address to Israel changes to the third
person and we leave behind the kings and princes. Nevertheless,
the continuity is there. God's indictment of Israel continues, and
the buildup towards the increasingly bitter threat continues. What
has changed is that we have moved from the particular to the
general: from sins of idolatry, sins of complacence and pride, sins
of the sinning kings, to "sin" and "iniquity" (or "guilt"). The verses
form a kind of summary. We may imagine that the charges have

been made in a court of law and verdicts have been passed on aspects of the case; now there is a pause, but the reason is not given. It is more than legal delay—maybe a hung jury, or an appeal, or time for amendment of life. Whatever the reason, there is a breathing space, an opportunity for one supreme effort (v. 13), a chance for the judge to muse (v. 14a, b). Meanwhile all the evidence is collected and filed (v. 12). Nothing will be overlooked when sentence is given; the record of wrongdoing is complete and in no danger of being lost. Job wanted the evidence to be recorded and preserved as testimony to his innocence (Job 19:23ff.); Ephraim's transcript would condemn him utterly. The records room of a law court gives way to the image of a mother in labor; but the central figure is not the mother about to give birth but the fetus Ephraim about to be born. The image occurs elsewhere (e.g., 2 Kgs. 19:3), where the concentration is on the mother and her inability, through lack of strength, to give birth. Hosea stretches our imagination to the full as he depicts baby Ephraim remaining in the womb, not because the mother is feeble but because the infant is stupid. This is not a stillbirth due to natural causes but one brought about willfully through foolishness. That the parable is impossible is irrelevant; its point is perfectly clear, and that is that Ephraim is both responsible and culpable. Faced with the choice between life and death, he has chosen death and made the womb his tomb. Two things are being said, and both of them coincide with the central themes of the chapter. First, Ephraim is without excuse. Even if he is not exactly committing suicide, the awful disaster that is about to come upon him is entirely his own doing.

The swords and spears may be Assyria's, and the overall plan and time of execution may be God's arranging. This in no way reduces Ephraim's responsibility. He will still die by his own high hand. The second lesson of the brief parable is that wombs can become graves and mothers executioners. The body which had chosen to give life and the cervix which exists to open wide that life might be enjoyed could also smother and strangle. God had conceived Israel (Hos. 13:4). He had nurtured her (vv. 5-6). Now was the time for Israel to choose life. But evil, insane Israel had chosen death. Now "mother God" would honor the choice and be the cause of death.

Questions abound when we come to v. 14, and one cannot claim total confidence in any answers offered. However, one's attempt to find satisfactory answers is greatly affected by the answers previously given to the structure of the chapter as a whole. Taken in isolation the verse presents more problems than if it is seen as part of a cohesive whole. We are following the latter path, and in consequence we shall find some of the answers provided by the context. Every one of the five lines presents a grammatical or philological question. Verse 14a, b can be translated as statements and then read as: "From the grasp of Sheol I shall ransom them. From Death I shall redeem them." Similarly lines 14c, d are not necessarily questions and can be rendered: "I am your pestilence, O Death! I am your plague, O Sheol!" In the final line (v. 14e) the word "compassion" translates a term whose meaning is uncertain.

Perhaps under the influence of Paul's understanding of the verse in 1 Cor. 15:55, and also no doubt affected by the Greek version, earlier commentators heard in the verse an emphatic reprieve for Israel. Tempted to destroy his foolish people, God resists the temptation as in Hos. 11 and declares he will ransom and redeem them. This interpretation cannot be ruled out and still has vigorous modern defenders, but on the whole the majority view supports the opposite, despite its unwelcome nature. No one wishes to believe that God can say "To hell with them."

Ephraim in 13:14 is still within the protective care of God. He has been brought through the dangers of pregnancy and is now offered life. This he refuses. So what is God to do: give him the life he has rejected, or respect his decision and let death and the place of the dead claim him? The words "ransom" and "redeem" describe actions on behalf of those who are helpless. Someone in chains, for example, cannot remove those chains; they must be struck off them by someone else. This is not the condition of Ephraim, according to Hosea. Ephraim has long been nurtured in the womb of God and offered life by God; life is there for the taking. Ephraim is not in the least helpless; he is willful, and by his own will has chosen death. Is God then to coerce him into accepting life? For God to pretend that Ephraim is helpless and then act to ransom him from the power of Sheol is, paradoxically, to go against his own nature of love; it would be limiting Ephraim's freedom and would be an abuse of omnipotence. God has no alternative but to let matters take their course. There will be no stay of execution. All that remains is to give the final command. This comes in the form of questions. But the intent is in no way questionable; it is imperative. The plagues of Death and the destruction of Sheol are the instruments of death, and it is these that are being called for. "Compassion is hid from my eyes." Is God blinded by his anger (v. 11), or in this case is justice allowed to triumph over mercy, and if so, had Hosea forgotten about 11:8, 9? God forbid that we should try to iron out every religious wrinkle—the face of the ancient of days is not smooth like a baby's—but let us look a little closer and consider the apparent awkwardness. The compassion is hid from God's eyes. But it is still there, and it will reappear and have the last word because he is "God and not human." In other words, this verse is only a part and not the whole of God's purposes. The whole story needs this part, but the story as a whole has a very different ending.

Seen just as part of the story, the verse contributes a great deal. We have already noted that it stresses God's respect for human freedom even when the particular human beings are rebellious, idolatrous, and *unwise*. Furthermore it states loudly that there is only one ultimate, unique authority in the universe and not a plurality of powers. Also it proclaims that death and hell are in some way God's servants, obedient to his command. What more then does this verse contribute if we see it as part of the greater whole? First we see it as a conclusion to what has gone before in that it tells us that the God of justice is as good as his word. He governs a moral universe, and allows people to reap what they sow. They are granted the dignity of being treated as responsible beings possessed of the divine right of being punished. This is valuable, but it is not all. As a conclusion it is, of necessity, in part determined by the past, but the whole story is more than the past or even the present. It inevitably includes the future. That means there are more and more conclusions yet to come which are built on this one; but these at the same time partially cancel this conclusion and partially transform it. Thus this conclusion leads to other conclusions and to its own transformation. It leads, of course, to v. 16, where the execution actually takes place. But it also leads to the final chapter, where Hos. 11:8-9 is vindicated because ch. 14 shows what lies beyond the destruction. In that chapter is the promise of redemption—a new conclusion which bathes 13:14 in a wholly new light. Thus it leads to Paul's use of Hosea's threat in 1 Cor. 15:55, which builds in turn on the greatest conclusion of all, namely the Cross and the Resurrection. This ultimate conclusion first explains Hosea's words by showing that they are a part of the central theme of Scripture—death/life, Cross/Resurrection, destruction/new creation. But that conclusion also cancels and transcends Hosea's words by putting them in their proper place. They are given lasting value as being somber heralds of great good news to follow; at the same time they are given no finality because ultimately the good news cancels them by transforming them.

13:15-16   It has become fashionable to translate Hos. 13:15a as the RSV does rather than as the Hebrew plainly states (cf. RSV margin). I propose to follow the original and translate "Though he may flourish among his brothers." In addition to the fact that this is what the original means, there is another reason for the decision. This translation not only fixes the section firmly within the pattern of "fall from grace," but it continues the motif with which the chapter begins. It starts with Ephraim's exaltation in Israel, which presumably means that it was his Israelite brothers who trembled when Ephraim spoke. This surely is a kind of "flourishing among his brothers." The flourishing referred to in v. 15 might be a later and different kind of flourishing, but the theme is the same. Hosea is fond of recapitulating his themes.

The prophet also recapitulates the theme of the east wind (12:1) but with a different significance. In ch. 12 Ephraim is chasing the east wind and does it all day long. He does this in the context of herding wind in general. Such an activity highlights his stupidity (cf. 13:13). But more importantly, it is Ephraim who is choosing to chase destruction, and that is something else similar to 13:13. In 13:15 the east wind is back again; but now, instead of Ephraim chasing the wind, it is the wind that chases Ephraim. Moreover the east wind is now identified with the LORD, and the choosing is now the LORD's choosing and not Ephraim's. The theological design is the same as in v. 14 and in many other places in the prophecy. First Israel in their sin and insanity choose a way of destruction; then God "honors" the choice, takes control, and makes the chosen madness into his chosen means of punishment. The roles are thus reversed. Pursuing Israel is now pursued, and the redeemer-God becomes pursuer and punisher.

As the verse continues, it recapitulates images found in 13:5: images of wilderness and water; and then those of 12:8: images of wealth. The destroying east wind, arising from the ambivalent

wilderness, dries up the water and "strips his treasury."
Countryside and city, agriculture and culture, all will be ruined.
This is actually what happened when Assyria became the wind, historically speaking. But to linger over that would be to fall prey to
a facile form of reductionism, for the wind's first cause was the
LORD — the ambivalent LORD. The same LORD who once
nourished his people *in* the wilderness now brings terror and mor-
tality *from* the wilderness. This reveals the same design and theology as the womb that suffocates in 13:13.

It is almost happening! The instant threats, judgments, warnings, verdicts, and sentences are about to become actual. The east
wind, the plague, the lion, the leopard, the bear are all about
Samaria. The outcome of the imminent attack is so predictable that
Hosea describes it in graphic and gruesome detail. As often in
Hosea, past, present, and future are bound together in a causal
bundle (vv. 1-3). The past is a history of rebellion; therefore the
present generation of adults and children shall be slaughtered, and
even the unborn are not exempt. There will be no future for guilty
Israel. This time it is both root and branch destruction. The verse
begins and ends with the common theme of Israel's total responsibility for what will happen. Of the three causes—God, Assyria,
and Israel—it is the last that is emphasized here. Samaria is guilty
because they have rebelled. So the verse begins. And then at the
end the theme of culpability returns only slightly disguised. What
happens to their own unborn offspring is only what Israel themselves had chosen (v. 13)—death in the womb.

This final verse of the chapter is about Samaria. Is there a special reason for not continuing to speak of Ephraim or Israel, or is
it merely a stylistic change? Certainly when the blow fell it was
Samaria that received the brunt of the attack, being besieged for
three years (2 Kgs. 17:5). Hosea perhaps anticipated this, but it is
likely that the use of "Samaria" here was quite deliberate. Most of
the sins which have been delineated earlier were particularly associated with the capital city. The kings were housed there, cultic
decisions made there, and political treaties arranged there. The city
was the powerhouse of rebellion and determined the rebellion's
direction. Like later Babylon and Rome, the capital was the heart
and head of the nation; just as its responsibility was greater, so was
its punishment.

A final question: What happened to Jacob? There is no clear

reference in the chapter to the patriarch. A possible link between Hos. 13:13 and Jacob in the womb (Gen. 25) has been suggested, but it is tenuous. And yet Jacob's shadow still looms large, for the wrestling Jacob of Gen. 32 is surely present in some way in the conflict between God and Israel in Hos. 13. Both Jacob and Israel are "exalted among brethren," both are elect, both have treasure, and both are in conflict with an ambivalent enemy who acts ambivalently. Ambivalence is a feature of both accounts. Did Jacob fight a man, an angel, or God? Did Israel fight their own harvest of wrongdoing, or Assyria, or God? As for God, is he friend or foe? He blesses Jacob but also fights with him and lames him. And to Israel God is both shepherd and lion, helper and destroyer. Is the later conflict merely a reflection of the original wrestling, or is there something new here? Is there even some development? Both in Genesis and in Hosea, the patriarch Jacob is said to have prevailed. This is certainly not true of Ephraim. Hosea insists that it is precisely the opposite: it is God who prevails and Ephraim who dies. Herein lies the great difference: for Jacob success, for Ephraim destruction. But this is not the end of the whole story. Beyond the end of Ephraim there is still Hos. 14 and Israel's healing. Then Ezekiel follows with Israel's resurrection, followed again by Isaiah's announcing Israel's comfort. The final chapter is the NT, with the coming of the One who is the glory of his people Israel and who through his death and resurrection establishes the New Jerusalem, whose tribal gates are built upon apostolic foundations. The whole story takes us through a death more momentous than that of Ephraim to a greater success than Jacob, the dreamer of heaven and angels, could have dreamed.

The difference between Jacob's story and Ephraim's lies in Ephraim's destruction. The development comes about through Ephraim's death, which mysteriously is the great advance. The great turning point in the whole long biblical story is Christ's resurrection; without that there would be no New Jerusalem. But conversely there could be no Resurrection without the death of Christ, for that was its necessary condition and preparation. In conclusion then, Jacob is still there in ch. 13, but he is now overshadowed because One greater than Jacob is also there. Ephraim's wrestling looks back to Jacob's but is not limited by it. Ephraim's is a greater struggle, greater because he does not prevail. In fact he fails, but in the failure he points to that mightier presence which is mightier than Jacob's. Jacob and Jesus are both there, but Jacob is decreasing as Jesus increases. Hosea, after all, is a prophet not only of the eighth century but also of the first.

UNREASONABLE REDEMPTION: GOD LOVES BECAUSE HE LOVES
Hosea 14:1-9

All my hope on God is founded

The move from ch. 13 to ch. 14 is like travelling from one age to another, or even from one world to another. We have become accustomed to Hosea juxtaposing good news with bad news. But nothing quite prepares us for the quick transference from the darkness of ch. 13 to the warm and brilliant light of ch. 14. And yet, in its own way, the book follows the common pattern of Isaiah, Ezekiel, Amos, and even Jeremiah in the Septuagint version, of putting the best news at the end. The pattern is wider even than the message of the prophets. Where we usually speak of night and day, Genesis tells of day and night, Exodus tells of bondage and liberation, and so on. It is almost as though the theme of death/resurrection is present in Scripture wherever we look and that Hosea is only echoing the dominant theme with his own extreme Galilean accent. Having said that, questions still remain. It may be that our understanding is bettered if we take the questions seriously and use them as a key to unlock the chapter. First we shall examine the contents verse by verse and then, having learned something of their meaning, ask how it relates to what has gone before.

I shall assume that 14:1-8 are a unity which is to be divided into three parts: vv. 1-3, 4-7 and 8. Furthermore, I see no reason to question that the verses are from the pen of Hosea. Whether Hosea wrote v. 9 is impossible to say, but the likelihood is small. Nevertheless, it belongs to the book and contributes more to the understanding of the whole book than to its immediate surroundings.

14:1-3 The form of vv. 1-7 is liturgical and consists of confession (vv. 1-3) and absolution (vv. 4-7). The first three verses consist of an imperative addressed to Israel (vv. 1, 2a) and the confession they are commanded to make (vv. 2b, 3). The command could come from either God or the prophet, more likely the latter.

The first word, in the Hebrew as well as the RSV translation, sets the tone for the chapter. It is the word "return" *(shub)*. The whole chapter is concerned with Israel's return to God, so the word serves as a kind of title. Furthermore, in one sense the word is not unexpected. It has occurred before (3:5; 6:1), where it expresses the great longing which Hosea (and God) has for Israel. If only they would do an about turn and return to God. So we may say that the word *belongs* at the beginning of the chapter, for if it were not there it might even suggest a lack of consistency. At the same time we ask, How can it be there? Has ch. 13 left anything at all that might be able to return? Is Israel not as good as dead? What is more, if there is indeed still a remnant, is God at all interested in it? After his attitude shown in ch. 13, could God care less? Right in the beginning, then, with the first word (which is v. 2 in the Hebrew) we have encountered the dilemma. The whole chapter centers round a theme which belongs in it as nothing else could, and yet from beginning to end we are astounded and questioning.

Whether it is the prophet speaking or God, the whole is all a word from the LORD, "the LORD your God," who made covenant with Israel and who is about to assure them that he still (wondrously) keeps covenant. The invitation to return and the words of confession take their meaning from and are validated by what follows in vv. 4-8. There may be three voices intended: the prophet's commanding, Israel's confessing, and God's declaring salvation. But in fact there is only one voice and that is God's, offering free redemption. The first verse is addressed to Israel, who has "stumbled" because of "iniquity." The "stumbled" refers back to ch. 13 and Israel's necessary death. There is no pretence, no ignoring the bleak reality of that punishing disaster and the rebellion that caused it. Just as the call to confession is based upon the assured salvation that is to be offered, so the new beginning, so freely offered, is strangely dependent on that terrible end and all that caused it.

The "stumbled" only looks backward. The "iniquity" too looks backward to the centuries of sin, but it also looks forward to the confession of that sin which begins in 14:2, and in particular to the details of it in v. 3. Verse 2, like v. 1, begins with a shock. Israel is bidden a second time to return to the LORD, and naturally, they cannot go to him empty-handed. There must be an offering in Israel's hand. This is to be expected, but what is totally unexpected is the nature of the offering. Israel is to take words! One's first reaction is that there had been no shortage of words and that, anyway, words come so easily. What about 6:1-3, where Israel did once already return with words, but with words so insincere that God had to use his own words to slay them? And did not God plainly say what he did want, and that was not words but "steadfast love" and "the knowledge of God"? We may wish to ask whether Hosea really means "words," as we remind ourselves that the Hebrew for "words" can also mean "deeds" or "events." But that God really does mean "words" is stressed in a variety of ways, including the unambiguous expression "the fruit of our lips."

The significance of taking "words" is very great. One might cynically say that Israel had nothing else to offer; and of course part of the meaning is that the sacrifices of the cult were no longer acceptable and that some alternative was essential. But much more is intended. Without denying the need for obedient action in the slightest, we may state that biblical faith is word-centered. It is based on what God has done. It is a story of events, a story that must be told. The events demand that they be witnessed to, in words. But plain narration is not sufficient. The events require interpretation, and that in turn requires foretelling and later — explaining. More words. The God of Scripture is a speaking God who says "Hear, O Israel" and "He who has ears to hear, let him hear," and who finally comes in his Son who is the Word incarnate. This speaking God, whose word is a two-edged sword — both creating and destroying — enters into a living relationship with those made in his image. It is a relationship between persons—soul with soul, will with will, and this demands language. Hosea, in earlier chapters, has documented a relationship of wrestling and conflict: Jacob and God, lion and prey, enemy and victim. This struggle is now at an end, he says. The relationship continues, but its nature is wholly changed. Now in sincerity soul meets soul, will meets will, lover meets beloved. For this words are essential. Sins are to be confessed, forgiveness proclaimed, faith affirmed, the beloved wooed. In place of the relationship of Jacobean wrestling, this new relationship is to be a dialogue rooted in steadfast love. Any dialogue needs words; this one needs them doubly.

The call for words is one of the signs in the chapter of a totally new beginning. Words had been important ever since the call of Abraham, but in the main the relationship had been dependent on institutions: the king and his court and his armies, but above all on the shrines and their sacrifices and priests. These institutions had outlived their usefulness, according to the prophet. Something totally new must take their place, and words somehow are at the heart of this new factor. For the external, institutionally-based relationship which resulted in so much conflict there is to be a more hidden basis—truth in the inward parts might describe it. But this would need some discernible expression, and its natural medium would be words. Scholars are uncertain when synagogue worship began. A common assertion is that it appeared first in the time of the Exile. Yet it might have started earlier, and even if it did not it could well have had roots in earlier convictions and experiments. Such worship which eventually replaced the sacrificial cult was word-centered. Did it owe its inception, in part, to these words of Hosea? Or was Hosea pointing to something already there in embryo?

The words first request that God "take away all iniquity." There is nothing to suggest that Israel or anyone among them except the prophet ever uttered this liturgy of penitence, which includes confession and renunciation. Israel was as good as dead and could not confess. But even if confession had been possible and these words were Israel's own, the people still acknowlege their inability to rid themselves of iniquity. The God who wills to save them from sin must not only furnish the formula of penitence; he himself must take away the iniquity. The next phrase, "accept that which is good," might be a still further embellishment of the "words" theme. Hans Walter Wolff translates "accept the word," on the assumption that the Hebrew term for "good" on occasion can mean "word" (*Hosea,* 231, 235). If this is correct, v. 3 includes four different ways of emphasizing this "words" theme. If God will take the initiative and take away iniquity, then Israel's response is "the fruit of our lips"—not the fruit of their flocks or fields, or even of their own loins in human sacrifice, but words confirming their sins and their faith.

If we take the RSV translation as it stands, it is possible that the phrases "Take away all iniquity; accept that which is good . . ." should then be linked with "take with you words" and "we will render the fruit of our lips." If we do this, then they become requests which apply to Israel's speaking rather than to their past actions. Israel is bidden to return to God, talking words. On the people's past record the chance of all those words being acceptable is very slight. It is far more likely that they would include words of nonsense, pride, and rebellion. This the liturgy allows for and asks God to sift what is offered, removing the bad and preserving whatever is good.

The liturgy continues with vows of renunciation that look to earlier chapters and provide a summary of Israel's wrongdoings. It takes the form of a trinity of sin. "Assyria" (actually 'Asshur') designates the country along with the god of Assyria, but here it represents Israel's rulers and the political maneuvers and errors of succeeding dynasties which have led God's people to trust in the gods of other peoples. Closely connected with "Assyria" are the "horses" (or 'chariots') which represent the cream of the fighting forces. The third item is the fundamental sin: the sin of idolatry. All these Israel is to repudiate, for it is these that had taken the people away from God; until these barriers are removed, Israel is unable to return to him.

Kings, army, and cult: what do they have in common, and how have these been responsible for Israel's death? First, they are all institutions and elements in Israel's society. In themselves they are good and valuable, but they exist in a corrupt form and so are pernicious and actually ruinous. On the surface two of them are secular and one is religious, but to Hosea they were all profoundly theological each in its own way and thus able to mislead Israel into ways of death. Three words indicate the common nature of their danger: "security," "adultery," and "idolatry."

The three institutions all offer differing kinds of security. This is obvious; what is not so obvious is that the three areas which they profess to secure were all the prerogative of God. He was the true king, the LORD of armies, and the source of that religious peace for which the cult existed. As God's servants the institutions were part of his blessing, but they gradually came to rival their master, not to serve him. The fatal three also represented identity. Unconsciously they either announced the sovereignty of the LORD they served or they broadcast his "poverty and weakness" once they had supplanted him in the eyes of the people. Thus not only was God's identity at risk, so also was Israel's. Israel was God's special creation, and their identity was inseparable from his. When he was worshipped as the Holy One of Israel, then Israel was a nation of priests, a holy people: God's inheritance. When God was no longer king and the kings took his place, Israel became a nation of slaves. When God was no longer the LORD of armies, Israel lost their security and became victims, first of their own leaders and then of the kings of the nation.

Ultimately all three institutions became idols and God was mocked. All this Israel now renounces; so the verse ends with the great therapeutic affirmation addressed to the world's lost and insecure and alienated. Kings, armies, and cults have robbed Israel of their security and identity and made the people into an "orphan." Orphans can do nothing to change their status or role. They are wholly at the mercy of others. This Hosea accepts and turns into a cause for thanksgiving. An orphan can be adopted by someone or, in this case, miraculously born again, "not of blood nor of the will of the flesh nor of the will of man, but of God" (John 1:13). Although they are orphaned and destroyed by sin, the prepared confession encourages Israel to "lift up their heads, because their redemption is drawing near" (Luke 21:28). At everyone's mercy, Israel is assured that in the God of Israel "the orphan finds mercy."

14:4-7 These verses are God's statement about Israel's future. They come in the form of a decree, communicated by the prophet, perhaps to his immediate circle of sympathizers. They would be heard, however, as originating in heaven and as first spoken in God's Council, which Hosea was privileged to attend that he might report its findings. The verses follow logically and spontaneously upon the confession, but their dependence is the other way about. Israel is called to confess and renounce because God decrees their salvation. Hosea 14:4 is crucial not only to this section but to the whole chapter, and perhaps the whole book. This verse describes the fundamental decision, while the following three verses describe what flows from the decision.

Three declarations announce the great turning point in Israel's fortunes. The last of them looks backward and gives the glad tidings that God's anger has turned from them. Israel has been called to turn, but the more significant turning is that of God's anger turning from them. This statement is the ground for the other two as those look forward. God is the physician who saves lives because life is his gift. Israel has rejected life by their apostasy, about which they can do nothing. But God can. He removes the fundamental problem, faithlessness, and he does this for the same reason that his anger turns away—because he loves Israel. This is a love which is free and spontaneous, finding its only reason in the character and disposition of the lover. It loves not because the lover has promised to love, nor primarily because he is moved by compassion for distress in the object of his love. Even less does it love because the beloved is lovable or offers anything in return. This love belongs only to God. God loves in absolute freedom. God loves because God is love.

The love theme has been struck, and the language of love continues. Similarities exist between this section and 2:14ff. There God is the wooer and fiancé and husband, and his love is grounded wholly in his own nature. This love is spontaneous and unconditional (esp. 2:19-20). Similarities also exist between 14:5-7 and the Song of Songs. Both anthems use nature imagery in the service of love. This extensive use of nature images is found in the book of Job and is common in most Wisdom Literature. This is a reason for not dismissing v. 9—obviously a wisdom saying—without careful consideration, on the grounds that if wisdom motifs are already present in the chapter, might the last verse not be earlier than is normally assumed.

The image of dew, used of Israel in 6:4, returns as an image of God's presence and influence. The meaning is now totally different. Used of Israel it signifies the cause of death; used of God it is the source of new life. Watered with God's dew, Israel has the beauty of the lily and the stability of the forest. The beauty moreover is lasting, not ephemeral; it is like the olive. The "fragrance of Lebanon" may refer to the numerous herbs and bushes that flourish in the forests of Lebanon. If so, the line leads into 14:7, where Israel the beloved returns and rests under God's shade. Israel's downfall had been caused in large measure by their search for security and identity. These they had sought for in institutions of their own making or of their own corrupting. Redeemed by God, they rest secure in his shade and find their identity in being his peculiar possession, his inheritance. They are his flowers, his trees, his oil, his fragrance, his garden (or his "grain," RSV margin). Finally they are a true "vine" (Isa. 5, 27), and their wine is likened to the vintage of Lebanon.

14:8-9   Hosea 14:8 can be translated quite differently (see, e.g.,
James M. Ward and Hans Walter Wolff). In particular, the substitu-
tion of "afflicted" for "answered" in the second line might be preferred. However, the RSV makes good and significant sense of the
verses, and so much that has gone before is comprehended in them
that they form a kind of summary. The first line goes to the heart of
the rebellion, namely, idols—idols of king, court, chariots, and cult.
These are the things Israel turned to for their security and identity
instead of turning back to God. Neither God nor Ephraim has any
connection with idols except the stance of bitter opposition. The
second line states the true reality: security and identity are found in
God and not in idols. In making the affirmation, Hosea echoes the
language and thought of ch. 2, where God states that it is he who
answers the pleading heavens as they have answered the pleading
earth (2:21). It is God and not the Baals who provides all they need
and whom they should thank (2:8).

Hosea 14:8 ends by likening God to an evergreen tree, the
source of Israel's fruit. What may be a horticultural abnormality
can be theologically illuminating, and this certainly is. It says that
God is enduring and unchanging, and that he is the source of
mankind's nourishment. It appears very straightforward until one
realizes that this is the only place in the OT where God is likened
to a tree; furthermore, trees are tainted for Hosea because they are
symbolically significant in the fertility rites (4:12-13). Are there
other conclusions to be drawn? It may be that we should first conclude that the book was designed to end with the tree of life theme
(Gen. 3:24) in a very bold form, namely that God himself was the
tree. This possibility is of course by no means ruled out, even if we
persist in asking whether anything more is intended. We have
noticed on our way through the chapter several references of
various kinds to elements in the earlier chapters. We have already
remarked above that the first part of Hos. 14:8 also does precisely
this. Is the explanation merely that an author cannot help leaving
his footprints wherever he walks, or is there something more
deliberate that contributes to the understanding of the chapter and
to the whole book?

Before attempting to answer this question, the final verse (v. 9)
must be examined. Maybe it has something to contribute. Does it
express merely "offensive," "easy piety" (Ward, *Hosea*, 228), tacked
on to mitigate Hosea's earlier offensive unpiety? Or is it an indica-

tion that one of the earliest interpreters of Hosea was already finding him heavy going? Or is Brevard S. Childs correct in seeing in the verse something that applies to the whole book? According to Childs, among other things the verse characterizes "the collection of Hosea's oracles on wisdom" and further emphasizes the metaphorical and symbolic value of the book for later generations within Israel (*Introduction to the Old Testament as Scripture*, 382).

I take the verse, whether it is by Hosea or by a later editor, to be "Hoseanic," in the sense that it uses Hosea's language ("transgressors," "stumble") and that it is designed also to comment on the whole book. It commends the book as "wisdom" for later generations, which means that it possesses teaching which in large part is liberated from its original historical roots and now functions parabolically and symbolically for those who trust in the God of Israel. Rooted in history and especially the saving history, it now blossoms and bears fruit in different times and different places. Indebted profoundly to the particular, it has become general, even universal. Its interpretation is not a matter of comprehending dates and facts and unrepeatable events. The task is far more difficult. Each generation must find the wisdom and discernment to understand the book and unlock it afresh; and such gifts come to those who know that the ways of the LORD are right and who discover that wisdom and discernment for themselves only through the fear of him. It is worth noting that this clear move from the particular to the general, from matter-of-fact to metaphor, is foreshadowed in the nature imagery which precedes the final verse. Nature is general; Jacob and the Exodus are very particular.

We return to the questions posed above about the meaning of the chapter and its relationship to preceding chapters, and we do it with some encouragement from v. 9. Does not ch. 14, by providing a conclusion and consummation to the whole book, therefore present us with a totality, a unity, and a wholeness which has hitherto largely escaped us? And are we therefore now able to hear new notes, or at least to hear more clearly notes that before were faint? And, with such new and clearer notes, are not some themes more distinct and the harmonies and dissonances more discernible?

We have already noted that moving from ch. 13 to ch. 14 is like moving into a new world, or like moving from darkness to light. The sense of surprise continues to be with the reader throughout the chapter as each verse produces something unexpected. How can God expect Israel to respond to the call to return? What is the use of returning with words? How can Israel summon sufficient willpower to renounce their sins? How can God's anger, so obvious in ch. 13, have evaporated so quickly? And, how can God's insistent demands that his conditions be met suddenly make way for love fully and unconditionally given? And how is dew, once a fatal sign, so transformed? And what about all the nature references? What has happened to the message once so inseparable from the saving history? And how can Hosea's polemic against the nature gods be reconciled with the description and images of 14:5-7? Finally, is the likening of God to a tree with its phallic, fertility symbolism not a climactic and final challenge to our credulity?

No pattern could fully comprehend such a variety as the above questions indicate, yet a faint design is discernible in what may be termed "ambivalence and transformation." The dew and the tree images are typical and illustrative of the design. The dew in ch. 6 is the symbol of a fatal disease in Israel; in ch. 14 it is the token of new life in God. The tree (or pole) of ch. 4 is the symbol of mordant apostasy; in ch. 14 it is the sign of God himself in all his enduring, nourishing power. It would seem that the whole chapter is witness to such ambivalence. The wrathful God has lost his anger; words that before were only mist are now firm and necessary; dangerous, seductive nature now mirrors God. Ambivalence is everywhere. But is ambivalence a pattern or category, or is it only a label for chaos and confusion?

Ambivalence may possibly signify ambiguity or indecision or craftiness, but this is unlikely in the present context. Hosea was not frivolous or venial; his ambivalence is of a weightier sort. Ambivalence may conceivably point to emptiness or meaninglessness; Hosea's ambivalence is testimony to that which is the source of meaning and all fulfillment. He, perhaps uncomprehendingly, spoke the words of the God who is both judgment and mercy, severity and compassion, wrath and love. Furthermore, Hosea prophesied in a time when there was a dual movement to be announced. There was a movement towards an inevitable judgment and punishment, but at the same time there was a greater journey towards forgiveness and healing. The second one is the redemptive journey—the movement from judgment to mercy, from severity to compassion, from wrath to love. Hosea tells the tale of both of these journeys.

The divine ambivalence which meets us everywhere in the book is how human understanding sees the all-comprehending God, and this meets us in many places in Hosea. Only when we arrive at the last chapter do we see the ambivalence at its clearest, because it is here that the true heart of God is most fully revealed—revealed in a movement away from what human eyes see to be its opposite. This is not so much a movement within God; God moves because he is moving Israel on a journey from death to life. The movement is a redemptive journey which reveals the ambivalence at its clearest but also fills it with most meaning because the movement is the giving of life. This meaning is not only explanatory. It is the meaning which is the source of all other meaning that is not judged but itself judges. As Israel is being saved, the whole nature and transforming power of God is exposed. Consequently all the ambivalence that is revealed is also shown to be an example of God's redeeming and transforming powers which can affect all things. As deathly dew becomes life-giving dew and phallic symbols become signs for God, so all creation is given hope because the God who appears as the God of contradiction at one level is demonstrated to be the God of salvation when seen at the deepest level. What we are speaking of has already been with us, even though less clearly, since ch. 1. The children of Hosea, for example, at the first are "not pitied" and "not my people," but they become "pitied" and "my people." The cultural elements most opposed by Hosea become his weapons, in a transformed mode, to bring about their own destruction. In 2:13 God is punishing Israel; in 2:14 he is wooing her. The contrasts are not so stark as they later become in ch. 11 and in chs. 13 and 14, but they are clearly there. The ambivalence is present because as people see God he appears in an ambivalent light. Seen in our categories and defined in our terms, God is wrath and love, judgment and mercy, source of death and source of life. But if we shine on the ambivalence a more prophetic light and see it in reverse from its future goal, then the ambivalence is seen as an inevitable aspect of redemption.

The ambivalence and redemption are shown to us in this book which is by an Israelite written for Ephraim and preserved by Judah. The book exists in part to combat the poisonous influences of an alien culture, to oppose any dependence on other nations, and to shatter the idols of the uncircumcised. Hosea was not internationally-minded or attracted in the slightest by "the wider ecumenicity." Words such as chauvinistic or even racist would be nearer the mark. He also shows no sign of a missionary call such as even Amos had. Despite this, he provides an abundance of material for mission thinking, not least in ch. 14.

For whom is the redemption intended? It is for Israel, obviously, but is it only for Israel? Who is the "orphan" in 14:3? If v. 9 opens the door to "whoever is wise," "whoever is discerning," then was it only Israel who could say the words of confession in vv. 2 and 3? And why, suddenly, is God defined not by those deeds which were known only to Israel but in the language of all nations which is common to all people? Is there a link with that missionary book Job, where the hero, a non-Israelite, is saved with no mention of the Exodus or Zion but with numerous references to God's work in nature? Does Hosea see so clearly the ambivalent, transforming God that, almost unknowingly, he prefigures Isa. 49:6 and hints that "it is too light a thing . . . to restore the preserved of Israel" and that he also is being given "as a light to the nations"?

We have shone the light of redemption onto the contradictions and ambivalence found in Hosea, but it has not been a very bright light. If we turn to the brightest light of all (for he is the light of the world), we find ready confirmation for much that we have said. The carpenter-king, the baby-God, the slaughtered Creator show us ambivalence writ large. We can echo the kings in Israel when they complained "Who has believed our report?" The ambivalence is beyond belief. Most unbelievable is that his death is death for all and his resurrection eternal life for all. In this light Hos. 14 and the whole prophecy become believable. Hosea is a true prophet. He points to the great contradiction, the ultimate ambivalence—the Word made flesh. At the same time, he and his prophecy are best understood when seen as part of a totality which witnesses to that other Galilean.

SELECTED BIBLIOGRAPHY

Andersen, Francis I., and Freedman, David Noel. *Hosea*. Anchor Bible 24 (Garden City, N.Y.: Doubleday, 1980).

Brueggemann, Walter. *Tradition for Crisis: A Study in Hosea* (Richmond: John Knox, 1968).

Childs, Brevard S. *Introduction to the Old Testament as Scripture* (Philadelphia: Fortress and London: SCM, 1979).

————. *Old Testament Theology in a Canonical Context* (Philadelphia: Fortress and London: SCM, 1985).

Emmerson, Grace I. *Hosea: An Israelite Prophet in Judean Perspective*. JSOT Supplement 28 (Sheffield: University of Sheffield Press, 1984).

Knight, George A. F. *Hosea*. Torch Bible Commentaries (London: SCM, 1960).

Mays, James L. *Hosea*. Old Testament Library (Philadelphia: Westminster and London: SCM, 1960).

Napier, B. Davie. "Prophet, Prophetism," *The Interpreter's Dictionary of the Bible,* ed. George A. Buttrick, 3 (Nashville: Abingdon, 1962): 896-919.

Rendtorff, Rolf. *The Old Testament: An Introduction* (London: SCM, 1985 and Philadelphia: Fortress, 1986).

Rudolph, Wilhelm. *Hosea*. Kommentar zum Alten Testament 13/1 (Gütersloh: Gerd Mohn, 1966).

Ward, James M. *Hosea: A Theological Commentary* (New York: Harper & Row, 1966).

Wolff, Hans Walter. *Hosea*. Hermeneia (Philadelphia: Fortress, 1974).